17⁹⁵

Cape Breton's Christmas

A Treasury of Stories and Memories

D1300186

"It just came to me now. Here we are, with our own home, our own land, two lovely children, good health, good food and good neighbours. This is the best Christmas I ever had. Ever, ever, ever!"

—Tessie Gillis
"Our First Christmas"

Cape Breton's Christmas

A Treasury
of Stories and Memories

Edited with an Introduction by
Ronald Caplan

Breton Books

Compilation © 2015 Breton Books

The back cover photograph and the photograph above are from Christmas Eve at the Holten Canadian War Cemetery in The Netherlands. The town of Holten is home to the graves of 1,393 soldiers, most of whom are Canadians, including Cape Bretoners, killed in battle in the final weeks of the Second World War. Since 1991, at Christmas, Dutch children gather at the graveyard and light a candle in front of every grave in remembrance of the sacrifices made for their liberation. The photographs are copyright © Steve Douglas of the British Grenadier Bookshop in Belgium.

The rights to all stories in *Cape Breton's Christmas* remain with the authors. They are published here with generous permissions. All royalties from sale of this book will be donated to the CBC Radio One project called "Light Up a Life"—a fundraiser for Feed Nova Scotia. **Acknowledgements continue on page 155.**

We acknowledge the support of the Canada Council for the Arts for our publishing program.

 Canada Council for the Arts   Conseil des Arts du Canada

We also acknowledge support from Cultural Affairs, Nova Scotia Department of Communities, Culture & Heritage.

NOVA SCOTIA
Communities, Culture and Heritage

We acknowledge the financial support of the Government of Canada through the Canada Book Fund for our publishing activities.

 Canadä

Library and Archives Canada Cataloguing in Publication

Cape Breton's Christmas : a treasury of stories and memories / edited with an introduction by Ronald Caplan.
ISBN 978-1-926908-34-2 (pbk.)

1. Christmas--Literary collections. 2. Cape Breton Island (N.S.)--Literary collections. 3. Canadian literature (English)--Nova Scotia--Cape Breton Island. 4. Canadian literature (English)--21st century. 5. Christmas--Nova Scotia--Cape Breton Island.
I. Caplan, Ronald, 1942-, editor
PS8237.C57C36 2014   C810.8'0334   C2014-906531-0
Printed in Canada

MIX
Paper from responsible sources
FSC
www.fsc.org   FSC® C103567

Contents

Our First Cape Breton Christmas

AN INTRODUCTION BY
Ronald Caplan

Having had the pleasure of gathering the memories and stories for *Cape Breton's Christmas*—it seems only fair that I begin by sharing a little Christmas memory of my own.

In our first days in Cape Breton—in the early 1970s—everything seemed new and like a second chance to make our own lives. From salted cod to the huge meals the local people called "a tea" to our being the centre of every visit with people constantly asking "And you like it here?" as though we might be leaving tomorrow. It was all new and sweetly awkward and meaningful, and our rural neighbours seemed so accomplished, welcoming, and full of grace. And we at the same time were trying to figure out a life for ourselves and how best to live it.

And then came Christmas.

Growing up, I never had Christmas, other than the celebrations tied to the school year—the pageant and songs, the decorated class-room, the gift for the teacher. In our home we had no tree, no tinsel, only the background Christmas songs enjoyed over the radio and the lights on some neighbours' houses and their tree lights seen through the windows. So the opportunity for making a Cape Breton Christmas was part of a new world for me.

We decided to have Christmas.

After all, we had our first child, four-year-old Tyana, and she was alert to the world around us, and our neighbours were certainly preparing for Christmas. So we put Tyana to bed one night with the promise of the next day's big event—The Trek for the Christmas Tree.

Living with the spruce woods practically at our door, we went out the next morning bundled head to toe, and Tyana picked a little tree. I sawed through the less-than-two-inch trunk with my new bucksaw and together we carried the tree back to the house. We decorated it with whatever we could find and make—paper angels and six-pointed stars cut from my parents' Chanukah cards, likely strings of popcorn and cutout nameless items from Tyana's crayon drawings, whole Christmas cards and perhaps a few toys. It was all so long ago.

And one way and another we celebrated Christmas.

Some days later, as the tree was losing its needles, I put away the ornaments, and I picked up the little tree and started for the door.

"Time to say goodbye to the tree."

I could see that Tyana was not happy.

"We'll have another tree next year."

Tyana said, "I want to come with you."

Once outside, she realized that I was about to burn the tree.

"Wait. . . ."

"What for?"

"I'll be right back."

And Tyana was gone, into the house. Time passed. I did not know what to do. A little tree stuffed with crumpled balls of paper, matches at the ready.

Tyana came back carrying a sealed envelope.

"I wrote the tree a letter."

She put the envelope in among the branches and stood back.

She said, "Okay."

And I set fire to the balls of paper, and to the tree. And the tree and the letter burned. After a while we went inside for hot chocolate. And we did not talk about it, not for a long, long time. She never told me what she had written, what the letter said. And I didn't ask. Many years later when I brought it up, she did not at first remember the tree or the letter. But I've never forgotten.

Our First Cape Breton Christmas

As *Cape Breton's Christmas* came together, I realized that it was not going to be an easy book. There are no elves and few mentions of Santa. And while there are many stories of joy and good humour and family love, I was struck by the less obvious stories, the darker and more challenging Cape Breton experiences, at home and around the world.

And then I looked more closely at the Front Cover—the photograph of the Christmas tree made of lobster traps and coloured ropes and huge fish tails. It was created by Lloyd Michael MacInnes and Claire Crimp as part of a charity Christmas-tree-making competition held for the St. Ann's Bay community. The glowing tree stopped me as I drove through the night, stationed as it was beside the Colouratura Fine Arts Gallery in Indian Brook. I took a few pictures and drove on. I knew immediately I had the cover for the book.

But afterward, putting the book together, I wondered whether all that darkness, that black night surrounding the tree, was in the best spirit of Christmas. It was certainly true to the book itself; despite the hilarity and joy, so many stories were of Christmas nearly lost and Christmas celebrated in the midst of war, and the economic challenges of Cape Breton. It took my friend and longtime co-worker Bonnie Thompson to point out that lights shining through the darkness are in the very best spirit of Christmas.

And living with that thought, I realized that the photograph spoke not only of the holiday season but of Cape Breton life. I was reminded that Christmas is the birth of a second chance for all of us. And more and more, that tender, vulnerable Christmas tree—determined to push back the darkness—made sense to me, and seemed just right.

Christmas Eve at Bernie's Bakery

Paul MacDougall

Imagine it's two a.m. on Christmas Eve day, fifty years ago, as we drive towards Whitney Pier. Nearly everyone in Sydney is sound asleep. Only two of the stacks from the steel plant are operating. Clouds of red iron ore dust mix with the newly falling snow, painting a rosy hue over the bright December moon. A lone taxi passes us in the subway, the concrete subterranean tunnel that connects Whitney Pier to Sydney proper. Turning left on Ferris Street we end up on Meadow Street, a small nondescript lane that runs parallel to Victoria Road. Halfway up the street, light streams out of the window of a rectangular shaped building.

We get out of the car and go over and peer in the window. A man and a woman are busy mixing up huge amounts of flour and water. The smell of a wood fire wafts down from above. We inhale the aroma. The woman inside, Mrs. Kokoski, sees us at the window and gestures for us to come in, out of the snowy night. The smell of yeast and bread rising is everywhere.

We start baking early on Christmas Eve, she tells us. Usually our day starts at five in the morning, and ends around two in the afternoon, but today we have to finish baking early. Why's that, we ask. Because the turkeys start coming around eleven. Turkeys, we say puzzled. Yes, the turkeys, for Christmas dinner. Everyone in the neighbourhood brings their turkeys here to cook in the big brick oven.

It's 2012 now and it has been about thirty years since a turkey has been cooked in the bread oven at Bernie's Bakery. The bakery has long been boarded up, the paint faded and the only evidence that the building was once one of the busiest bakeries in all of Cape Breton is the vestige of an old worn-out sign still found above the door.

But back in its heyday they used to cook up to seventy-five and sometimes a hundred turkeys on Christmas Eve afternoon. Mrs. Kokoski started the practice simply in order to work in the bakery on this very busy day, and still get her turkey cooked in time for Christmas. Over time, relatives and friends got into the act, then customers, and eventually, anyone in Sydney who wanted the convenience of cooking their bird in advance of the Christmas rush made their way to the bakery early in the day.

Angeline Giacomantonio of Lingan Road remembers her husband Jimmy taking the turkey to Bernie's because she was busy all day baking her own sweets and Christmas goodies. Having the Kokoskis cook the turkey was a big timesaver back then. Currie MacDonald, a long-time resident of Whitney Pier, remembers the stream of people heading to the bakery with their turkeys every December 24th.

The turkeys all had a metal tag attached, to avoid mix-ups, and were put in the oven around eleven in the morning. The staff usually started around two in the morning on Christmas Eve, in order to finish baking by eleven. The turkeys were basted a couple of times, and were ready by three or four in the afternoon. If you couldn't pick up your turkey, then someone from the bakery would deliver it to you. The brick oven took four days to heat up and would stay hot for days. Morning temperature reached 550°F and leveled out around 350°F later in the morning.

The tradition grew over the years and would have continued except modernity got in the way. In 1980 a new oven was put in place and its racks simply couldn't take the weight. Close to two decades after the last turkey was cooked at Bernie's, people still used to call and ask if they could take their turkey over to cook. But the sights and smells of the little home-grown bakery on Meadow Street, which were such a delight to its hundreds of customers, no longer waft through the Pier.

We're back fifty years again, and the snow has stopped falling. A reddish colour marks the skyline. It's around eleven in the morning and the last of the Christmas bread has just come out of the oven. People are buying up everything in sight. The home-made square pizza is snapped up as soon as it hits the cooling racks. The door opens, and with a gust of cold wind, in comes a little man carrying the first turkey. It's a twenty-pounder. Everything is exactly on time, everyone is pleased. It's Christmas Eve at the bakery and everything is just right.

Better Not Pout

Jordon MacVay

It was Christmas Eve, 1958, their second year in the new house on Lorne Street. My grandparents, Duncan and Mary Theresa, were much more comfortable in the new house since Mary Theresa had already given birth to eight children. One of them, Hugh, had died in infancy, but the other seven were growing and thriving and required quite a bit of space. And there would be two more in the next few years, both boys, one of them named Hugh after his late brother.

Giving birth to all those children and raising them must have been a heck of a lot of hard work for my grandmother. My grandfather had to work hard at the steel plant, too, as the children needed not only adequate space but also food and clothing. And when Christmas rolled around, they needed presents.

Throughout the year, Duncan and Mary Theresa had bought the kids' Christmas presents bit by bit, one at a time, whenever they had a bit of money. They'd buy them at Crowell's and Eaton's and other stores along Charlotte Street, usually getting each one on layaway and making small payments. When Christmas was just around the corner they'd finally paid for everything, and were keeping all the items from the various stores in three boxes in the back room of one of the stores on Charlotte Street.

The store's deliveryman, it had been arranged, would bring the boxes around to Lorne Street on Christmas Eve, so the children would have presents to open on Christmas Day. This pleased Duncan, who'd been poor growing up.

With a winter storm raging outside, Duncan worried about his delivery, and worried even more as each hour that passed brought no sign of the deliveryman. Finally he decided to call the store. The phone rang and rang. Maybe they're busy, he thought. It was Christmas Eve after all. But there came a point when he realized the phone kept ringing not because everyone was busy, but because everyone had gone home. The store was closed. It was Christmas Eve, after all.

Duncan went for the phone book, splashed the pages around, found the cashier's phone number. Good thing he knew her last name. She was surprised to hear from him. The deliveryman, she told him, had already finished his rounds for the day and had gone home. Wasn't there anything she could do? The kids needed their presents. There wasn't . . . well, she could give Duncan the store manager's number. Well that was something. Duncan thanked her, wished her a Merry Christmas, and hung up.

When Duncan called the store manager's house, a woman answered. She was even more surprised to hear from Duncan, who she didn't know, than the cashier had been. Her husband, she told him, was out at a Christmas party somewhere. Wasn't there anything she could do? The kids needed their presents. There wasn't . . . well, she could try to get in touch with her husband at the party. Well that was something. Duncan thanked her, wished her a Merry Christmas, and hung up.

Duncan sat by the phone for a long time. The kids were already in bed, fast asleep, or at least in bed, thinking about Santa Claus and presents and watching the snowflakes falling past the streetlights. Duncan watched that same snow falling past those same streetlights but had no visions of Santa Claus trying to stuff himself down the chimney. He knew who was supposed to put the presents under the tree. He watched the snow falling and could see where it ended up. It was blown down and across and ended up in big drifts against the house. Every time he looked away from the phone, the drifts were bigger.

At one o'clock in the morning, the phone rang. Duncan pounced on it, as if the second ring would have set off a bomb. At the other end was a woman's voice. It was the store manager's wife. Her husband, she told him, had finally called her back. He would meet Duncan at the store. Duncan thanked her, wished her a Merry Christmas, and hung up.

He looked out the window, but he wasn't thinking about the huge snowdrifts that were squeezing the house. Instead, he was wishing he had a car.

Several minutes later, Duncan was in the passenger side of his next-door neighbour Benny Woodill's car. Benny had to work hard to keep the car from wiping out, not least because most of the way from Lorne Street to Charlotte Street was downhill. Benny jerked the wheel left and right, fighting with it, at times lifting off the seat, almost standing. Duncan slid back and forth across the big front seat, holding on to the door, his knuckles as white as the snow whipping the windshield. And then: Victory. They reached the store. But Benny's car was the only one in sight. Charlotte Street was empty, save for the thick coating of snow that made it hard to distinguish the road from the sidewalk. The only clue was a set of dull indentations that ran up and down the street, proof that cars had come by at some point.

At about one-forty-five a set of lights quivered around a faraway corner and swerved down the street towards the store. The car was newer than Benny's but had just as much trouble crawling along the doughy landscape. When it finally reached the store, the car slid to a clumsy, jerking halt almost on top of Benny's car. It took a few moments for the driver to get the door open. When he did, he climbed out and proceeded to stagger all the way to where Duncan and Benny were standing. There was a lot of snow, so the staggering was understandable. Duncan and Benny understood it more properly, though, when the store manager got close enough and they could smell the liquor off him.

The store manager, half-cut because he'd just left what was apparently quite a party, mumbled to himself as he fumbled with a big ring of keys for several moments, finally finding the right ones. Duncan and Benny followed him inside, all the way to a back room, where a ladder led to a small loft. That was where the boxes would be. The manager climbed up, slipping once or twice, and peered into the darkness of the loft. "Nope," he said, "nothing there."

Duncan felt a blast of heat run upwards from his chest to the tips of his ears. "What?! They gotta be there! I'm telling you, there were three boxes, and they. . . ."

"Hold on, hold on," said the manager. "Get me my flashlight. It's in the car."

Moments later, Benny came running back in, tracking half the storm in behind him. He handed the flashlight up to the manager, who clicked it on and held it at the entrance to the loft. "Ah," said the manager. "Now I see something. Three boxes, right? Well there they are, way at the back."

The manager crawled down to the back and dragged the boxes, one by one, to the entrance, then started to hand them down to Duncan and Benny. Finally, Duncan thought, now all we have to do is get home and get these presents under the—

"Hey!" A deep voice bellowed into the store, followed by the light of another flashlight, much brighter than the one the store manager was holding.

Duncan and Benny each put a hand up to their faces and squinted into the light that was coming from the store's entrance. It got closer, brighter, until a figure emerged. Before they could even discern any features, both men could recognize the shape of a police officer's hat.

"Hey!" the cop yelled again, finally coming into full view, his flashlight flicking back and forth between Duncan and Benny. "What's going on here?"

"We're getting my kids' presents," said Duncan.

"Oh are you now?" the cop chuckled. "And why didn't you just come here during the—"

"Okay boys, here's the last one!" It was the store manager, popping out of the loft entrance with the third box.

"Jesus, how many of you are there? Get down here, you!" The cop wasn't laughing now. As the store manager made his way down the ladder, the cop kept his flashlight trained on Duncan and Benny. "You two keep your hands where I can see them!"

"So," he said to the store manager, "I suppose you were up there getting Christmas presents for your kids, were you?"

"Oh no," the store manager said, the smell of alcohol escaping in all directions, "these presents aren't for my kids. They're for his." He pointed at Duncan.

"Oh," said the cop to Duncan, "so you're the ringleader here, huh?"

"Look," Duncan said, "this guy's the store manager. His deliveryman forgot to deliver the presents I bought for my kids, and it took me all night to get hold of him, and he came down here in this storm to meet me so I could get these presents. Now my kids are home in bed and when they wake up in a few hours these presents have to be waiting for them under the tree."

"I want to see some ID," said the cop. The three men pulled

out their wallets and produced cards, which the cop checked one by one. He looked at each man for several long moments, taking a few extra moments to study the face of the store manager.

"You two each take a box," the cop said to Duncan and Benny. He looked at the store manager, then bent down and picked up the third box himself. Then, turning to Duncan, he asked, "Which car is yours?"

Once the store was locked and the engines started, the men prepared for the long drives back home. Duncan paused before climbing back into Benny's car. "Thanks a lot," he said to the cop, who was rocking the store manager's car, trying to dislodge it from the mounds of snow that had crept up around it.

"Well," the cop said, while watching the manager's car swerve down Charlotte Street, "it is Christmas Eve, after all."

The drive back to Lorne Street, which was mostly uphill, took much longer than the drive down to the store. It took Duncan until five o'clock in the morning to get the presents under the tree. Each present had the name of a child who had long ago been lulled to sleep by the snow falling past the window and thoughts of Santa landing on the roof with his sleigh and his eight reindeer. It wasn't much longer before the seven children—including my mother—were standing in the living room, rubbing their eyes, about to dive at the tree and look for the presents that had their names on them, the presents Santa Claus had quietly left there while they were sleeping.

The family would go through some pretty hard times in the years to come. But those are all stories for another day. For now we'll leave the children, laughing and tearing open their presents, as their father looked on, tired and grumpy but still, when all was said and done, having a very Merry Christmas.

Our First Christmas

Tessie Gillis

I woke with a start. The bedroom was full of shadows. A few hours ago, when I blew out the lamp, it had been pitch dark. Now I could make out the shapes of drawers and even the clothes rack across the room. Heavy clouds had hung low over the Glen all week, dumping their cargo of white snow. But the clouds had gone away while we slept, and now the moon hung high in the sky and the countryside was bathed in light. It seemed like a miracle.

I heard footsteps on the landing.

"Jim," I whispered. "Wake up! The kids are up. I'm afraid Sonny might fall on the stairs. Those stairs are dangerous." I found myself shaking my head and mumbling. "We'll have to find the money somewhere for a banister."

Every day since the children had come I'd worried about the stairs, and I used to like how narrow and steep they were.

"What time is it?" said Jim, shaking off my arm. "What's the matter with them?"

"It's Christmas, remember? They are looking for the presents Santa brought. It's four o'clock. You'd better hurry if you want to see their faces."

The floor was ice cold. I'd have to get the fire going right away.

"Be right there," said Jim, as he jumped out of bed and pulled on his trousers.

Together we tiptoed down the stairs, through the kitchen and into the front room. Two small figures in long flannelette nightgowns stood silent and still before the Christmas tree. The moonlight reflected from the ornaments and the tinsel on the tree created an aura about them.

"Angels!" Jim whispered.

I lit the lamp with shaking hands. The tree Jim had chosen was much larger than the ones we used to have in our little apartment in New York, and the decorations we'd brought with us were too few for such a large tree. The stores in Port Hood didn't carry anything so frivolous, and it was too late for a mail order when we came to decorate the tree. But Anne and Sonny couldn't see anything wrong.

"Look, Daddy!" I still pretended to be surprised. "Doesn't this big doll look like Anne? Do you suppose Santa meant it for her?" Anne's eyes were like blue whirlpools.

"I don't suppose Santa would leave a doll for a boy, now, do you princess?" said Jim, lowering himself on his hunkers and putting his arm around her.

I took the doll from beside the tree and held it up. Anne chuckled with laughter, held out her arms, clutched the doll and held it close. It was nearly as tall as she was. I looked at Sonny.

"What did Santa bring for my big boy, I wonder?"

Sonny wasn't listening. He was looking at the tree.

"Look, Sonny, look! A fire engine! All for you. A big red fire engine!" Still Sonny paid no attention. Then suddenly he put out his hand and touched a golden ball hanging from the nearest branch. The ball quivered for a moment, then crashed to the floor, and shattered into tiny pieces. The corners of his mouth began to droop. But before Jim or I had time to speak Anne threw down her doll, grasped a blue and silver bell, threw it down on the floor, and danced up and down with glee.

"Anne! You musn't touch," I gasped, drawing her away. "They're not toys to play with. You mustn't touch the tree. Just look at the pretty things."

With two of the biggest ornaments broken, our poor tree

looked bare and forlorn. Jim took Anne by the hand and led her over to the armchair. He pointed to the bulging stockings hanging from either arm. I grabbed a small bear that stood guard over Sonny's stocking and held it close to his face, trying to block his view of the tree. Slowly his eyes began to sparkle through the tears. Then holding out his little hands he took the bear and held it close to his chest. He laughed. This was the first time I had ever heard him laugh. The fire engine lay unnoticed under the tree. I got up from my knees and touched my man-child on the head. Then I made my way out to the kitchen.

During the week between Christmas and the New Year every family in the Glen went visiting. Every man had to treat his neighbours to a drink. We would have to make at least two excursions—one up the road to the Beatons' and the MacTavishes' and the other down the road to Jim's father's place, Dougall's, J.J.'s, then up to Lawlors', and Ronnie's place over the hill. Jim thought we should start our visiting down the Glen. He harnessed Silver to the wood sleigh while I collected the old coats and comforters we had and piled them on behind. While I put on Sonny's coat, Anne had taken one of the last ornaments left on the tree and insisted on hanging it on Silver's bridle. Jim waved away my protests and we took off in a whirl of snow. The mare was well fed and eager to run. As we turned off the Settlement Road we could see that there was no smoke coming from the chimney of Jim's father's house. They too must be visiting. We continued on our way down the river until Dougall's house came into view. No smoke came from his chimney either and there were no children playing in the yard.

"We'd best turn around and go back up to Lawlors'," said Jim, "they're all over at J.J.'s and drunk by now." He turned Silver around in the next gateway and we retraced our way up the hill and on towards Lawlors'. Our call at Lawlors' was a duty call, for Charles Lawlor was the big man up our end of the Glen. His house stood well back from the road and guarded by a carefully clipped spruce hedge. It was painted white; the only painted house for miles around. We swung in past the painted high-barred gate into the driveway. Silver took the turn with a burst of speed then slowed down to a walk up the steep slope to the house. Soon we heard singing. A Gaelic song—I knew the tune . . . "They had neither pole nor paddle/ So they could not cross the stream." Then a man's voice rang out, more heartily than melodious, describing the hero's frantic efforts to cross the water to the accompaniment of clapping hands beating out the rhythm. Then once again many voices joined in the chorus.

Margaret Lawlor met us at the door. She clasped the children in her arms and swept us into the parlour. She was a gentle soft-spoken little woman with twelve children of her own. We had barely time to take off our coats and rubbers before glasses were pressed into our hands. At Lawlors' each guest was given an individual glass. In the kitchen was a gleaming stove hot from anthracite coal, and the air was filled with the aroma of spices from trays of cookies and cakes cooling in the pantry. Plates of turkey and pork sandwiches were laid out on long tables under the window. I was overwhelmed by the joy and hospitality around us. It was as if the framed blessing and prayers on the walls had all been brought to life. It was hard to believe, looking at Charles Lawlor now, that he could silence any one of his children, grown man or child, with a look.

The front room had been cleared for dancing. There was no musical instrument, but that didn't deter the dancers. As soon as a set finished, a voice started a faster tune, and before eight bars were sung the rest of the group joined in. A big strapping youth was pushed into the centre of the floor. He started a series of intricate steps. His feet moved like quicksilver, but his body remained rigid and his arms stiff. Soon our little Anne was jumping up and down trying to dance, and young Charlie Lawlor, a hefty lad in his early twenties, led her on to the floor. She didn't know any of the tunes, but she had a good sense of rhythm. I was so proud of her. She looked so pretty, and her red-gold hair gleamed as her partner held her up and spun her round and round. I was so glad that I had been extravagant and made her a party dress especially for Christmas. It was blue velvet with lace collar and cuffs.

No one seemed to get tired, and no one got drunk. Three times we tried to leave but Margaret Lawlor wouldn't hear of it. At last I managed to convince her that we would have to be on our way. The whole family came to the door to see us off. They jammed the porch, waving their arms and calling out, "Merry Christmas! A Happy New Year!"

"Wasn't that something?" I said, as Silver took off at a sharp trot.

"Aye!" said Jim. "Stayed longer 'n we should have."

"What a fuss Margaret made when I wanted to leave."

"Awful nice people," Jim replied.

We had one more call to make.

"It'll have to be hello and good-bye at Ronnie's," said Jim. "Sun's losing her heat and it'll soon be dark. Don't want to be stumbling round in the dark feeding cows."

Jim pulled Silver's rein sharply to the left of the road. The mare knew her way home and wanted to turn the other way. Reluctantly she climbed up to the brow of the hill. At the crest we could see Ronnie's house.

"Look!" I cried. "They're all out in the snow."

"Fightin'," said Jim. "Must be the Roosters. Christina's people."

"The Roosters?"

"Aye! The Roosters!" said Jim with contempt. "When they're around, there's feathers flying. There's a whole settlement of them down the road from the church. With no one around to fight, they fight they selves . . . and with anything that comes handy . . . fists, chairs, clubs, hair-pulling, anything at all."

"Let's not go in, Jim. We can wave from the road and turn

17

around at the church. They'll never remember."

"No!" said Jim. "Can't do that. And I don't want to make another trip over—special. Get it over now."

Inside the house, everyone was drunk, even the women. There was no sign of tea or any food. The men stopped fighting long enough to take the drink Jim offered them. One was passed out on the floor. We hadn't bothered to blanket Silver, and we left as quickly as we could.

"None of them will remember we were there," I said petulantly. "We should have gone past."

"WE know," said Jim, firmly.

"Do we have time to run in and give old William Barnes a drink?" I said, looking at the tall gaunt house that hadn't a single light shining through the windows. "It's Christmas, and that poor old man probably won't have any callers at all."

"We'll do that," said Jim. "We'll stay long enough to give him a drink, and that's all."

The children were fast asleep and warm. I went into the house while Jim tied up the mare. The old man didn't hear me enter the kitchen. He sat huddled over the stove, wrapped in an old ragged coat, a cap pulled down over his ears, and his booted feet in the oven. The whole room was hazy with smoke that poured from a crack on the stove top and a loose connection in the chimney pipe. The window was shrouded with limp shreds of curtaining that showed traces of having once been crisp and gay. An unlit lamp, the bowl empty and the funnel caked in soot, a grimy glass of water, and a flickering lantern stood on the table. The old man neither heard me, nor seemed to see me as I moved around.

"Don't shut the door," I called out to Jim when I heard his steps in the porch.

"Why the hell not?" Jim called back. "Want to freeze everyone out?"

"Leave it open. Just for a minute to let the smoke out."

As the air cleared, Jim looked around. I saw him looking at

the place beside the stove where marks on the wall showed that wood had been stacked there in days gone by. On the floor lay a single piece of wood, about two feet in length and an inch in diameter. I raised the lid of the stove and motioned Jim to look. Inside, a half-burned chunk of wood encrusted with mud lay smouldering. Jim bent down and shook the old man gently, then took the bottle out of his pocket and held it up for him to see. The old eyes grew wide with excitement. He drank thirstily, but when we shouted "Merry Christmas," he only laughed foolishly, his eyes blank and without expression.

"He doesn't know he's alive," I whispered.

"He don't have any wood," Jim whispered. "Must be some, some place."

"Doesn't he have any relatives?"

"There's a nephew or cousin or something in the village, but they don't pay him no mind. Never come out to see how he's doing. I'll take a look around and see if I can find wood for tonight."

Jim stopped at the door.

"Now we can't take him home, so don't try and be a Florence Nightingale, or something. Tomorrow, maybe, we can do something else . . . even if he is so mean that he wouldn't give his mother a nickel, and her starving to death."

"But we can't leave him to die alone at Christmas!" I protested.

"Now you stay here. I won't be a minute," said Jim, as he went out.

I picked up the lantern and found the pantry. The shelves were bare. There was no bread, nothing in the house. Jim soon returned with an armful of odds and ends of wood.

"Make him a cup of tea," said Jim, throwing the wood into the stove.

"I can't, Jim. I've looked everywhere and there isn't any food in the house. Not even a pinch of tea. It's too late to go home and get some, but we can leave the fruitcake and apples that are in the shoe box on the sleigh."

We left the cake and the apples with old William. Silver needed no urging, she was anxious as we were to get home. The sun had just disappeared over the far hills, and the light was fading fast. Jim would have to feed the animals by lantern light.

We heard the sleigh bells ahead before we saw Charlie Lawlor, standing spraddle-legged on his sleigh, towering over his mare. Jim hailed him, and reined Silver to a halt. We told Charlie what we had seen.

"Hmmm!" said Charlie. "D'ye think if I took him some potatoes and turnips, he'd have the sense to cook 'em? I'd best take a run up anyways."

"Well, that's our good deed for today," I said, as the sleigh moved off.

"If the neighbours are true to form, by the time Charlie makes his rounds tonight the old man'll have everyone in the Glen calling with their hands full before the week's out," said Jim, giving Silver a flick with the reins.

"What makes you think that?" I asked.

"Oh! Guessin'!" said Jim with a broad smile. "Margaret Lawlor'll make it her business to see that the relatives find out that the neighbours are feeding poor William, and they'll find a way of getting him away—him having all that money. I didn't see hide nor hair of his old dog. He must've breathed his last."

It was good to get home. I was cold and tired. What a Christmas it had been! I put the children to bed while Jim unloaded the sleigh and fed the animals. I soon had the fire going and the kettle singing on the stove. I looked out of the kitchen window. There was a full moon, and the snow was bathed in golden light. I could see Jim's lantern moving inside the barn.

"Mary! Come here!" It was Jim calling. "I got something to show ye!"

I pulled on my coat and boots, and ran out into the barn.

"Look!" said Jim, pointing to a heap of straw.

There stood a newborn calf, as frisky as a speckled trout. As soon as he saw me he darted over to his mother, old Star, who stood there, placid and content, chewing her cud.

"No need to ask is she all right," said Jim, throwing her an extra ration of hay. "Been a while since that feller came. Must've happened an hour or so after we left."

"Oh Jim! Isn't he a beauty! He's the best Christmas present I ever had. But I have something better than any gift this Christmas, Jim."

"An' what's that?"

"It just came to me now. Here we are, with our own home, our own land, two lovely children, good health, good food and good neighbours. This is the best Christmas I ever had. Ever, ever, ever!"

"The chaos, the cussing . . . it must be Christmas"

Ann Dempsey

My cousin Warren, a thirty-two-year-old father of three, stands in the middle of the family room, wearing . . . a fur coat? No, it's a crop of chest hair so thick you'd swear he killed a bear and slung the pelt over his shoulders.

Warren is shirtless, with a toy guitar around his neck and a child's bicycle helmet perched on his head. He's performing his Christmas classic, an extra sexy karaoke rendition of the Pussycat Doll's 2005 hit "Don't Cha." Gripping the microphone, he rubs his doughy middle section and belts out the lyrics. "Don't cha wish your girlfriend was hot like me?"

Welcome to Christmas Eve in Louisdale, the tiny Cape Breton village I call home, though I haven't actually lived here since I was eighteen. It's a French-Acadian community on the island's southwestern coast, pretty much in the middle of nowhere. Mass is over and we're all gathered at cousin Warren's house—my parents, kid brother, a gaggle of aunts and uncles, cousins wee and grown.

The children, far from nestled snug in their beds, run around in circles, stomping and banging and clanging like the Whos down in Whoville. All the noise, noise, noise.

Upstairs, the kitchen is a mess of empty pie tins, lasagna pans, cookie trays, wine and beer bottles—a feast enough to feed a small village, devoured in under an hour.

Before you ask, no, cousin Warren is not drunk. He's probably had a beer or two, which is all it really takes for anyone in my family to let loose.

And before you judge our taste in music, let me assure you we are well aware that our karaoke song list is limited. We lament the selection every year, but never think about updating it until it's too late. And so every Dececember 24 we pick up the microphone and belt out the same set of Shania Twain tunes and Top 40 hits of the early 2000s. It is enormously fun.

At twenty-six, I have not missed a single Christmas at home, most spent with my mother's family here in Louisdale. Despite lengthy stints abroad and moves halfway across the country, I have always made it back to spend the holidays with my family. There is nowhere I would rather be.

I've often wondered how outsiders would fare in our midst, and this year I will find out. My boyfriend is coming home with me for Christmas, which raises some interesting questions, including: will he make it out alive?

More importantly, when the shit hits the fan—pardon my

language—as it does so often and so spectacularly in my family, how will he react?

At the celebration a few years ago, my cousin Josh, who was six at the time, stuffed so much fruit into his mouth that he projectile puked an entire belly's worth of Christmas feast across the living room, prompting a stampede as those of us with weak stomachs gagged and swore and dove out of the way.

And then there was the year of the moose sausages, courtesy of cousin Warren, who happens to be a champion hunter. Were it possible to get a Ph.D. in hunting, Warren would not only have one, he would be in charge of awarding them. Ask him about hunting and Warren will show you his trophies—albums full of dead animal photographs. Dead ducks stacked in freezers, slain deer skinned and hanging from a tree, coyotes strung up by their hind legs in his shed.

But I digress. Back to the moose sausages. Cousin Warren tried to convince anyone who would listen that they were actually whole moose penises. Except he wasn't using a polite word for penis.

Nothing about my family is polite. We embrace vulgarity, even at Christmas. Especially at Christmas. Will my out-of-town guest tame the crowd? Not a chance. My family behaves for no one.

In the early days of my parents' relationship, my mom invited one of her sisters over to meet a friend of my father's family who was visiting from Halifax. She gave her sister, Valerie—my *tante*, as we call our aunts in these parts—strict instructions to be on her best behaviour. Tante Valerie is a notorious fountain of expletives and sometimes needs these warnings.

When the day came, my mom jokingly introduced the family friend as a priest. Tante Valerie gasped. "Eff off!" she said, meaning, of course, "No way! Really?"

This happened one Christmas in the 1980s. Later that day, in the living room, Tante Valerie complimented my mom on her poinsettias. "My god Anne Marie," she said, "what beautiful placentas these are."

Perhaps you have to experience all of this first-hand to understand and appreciate it. If that is the case, this week is sure to be a crash course for my boyfriend.

I don't expect him to run for the hills—I wouldn't be taking him home if that were the case—but I am very much hoping he will be able to make sense of and appreciate the way my family operates. And that he'll rock out at Christmas Eve Karaoke.

I suppose the bigger challenge will come when I am ultimately forced to spend the holiday season away from home. Will I make it through a Christmas without my family's unique brand of chaos? Truth is, I never want to find out.

A Curtis Family Memory

I used to be in the choir one time, *Helen Curtis told us,* and Jimmy used to sing in that choir. Oh, I can remember Christmas night, him and another teacher sang. They sang the "Adeste Fideles"—it's a beautiful, beautiful Christmas carol. I thought it was the beautifulest thing I ever listened to. Oh, I love it. Don't you love music? (*I love music. But you know, it's only as I grow older that it more and more touches my heart.*) Yes. Now, I love, love, love. *Helen thumps the table.* Sometimes when I'm alone—I'm here alone in the night, and I'll kind of get a little—if I'm not knitting, or doing some kind of work like that . . . I'll pick up one of those songbooks, and I'll sing and sing and sing and—go over those songs. And you know, I don't do a bad job on it, for all! And I don't seem to get tired. . . .

Monica McNenly, Helen's daughter: Our home was so close to the church that many, many people who came a distance to church came to our house, and were often put up overnight on a Saturday night so that they could go to church on Sunday. And I recall—and I suppose everyone in my family would recall—Christmas Eve, when people came from everywhere around to go to Midnight Mass. My father would let the animals out of the barn to make room to put the horses in so they could keep them warm while people waited to go to Midnight Mass. And they sang then. Before Mass. Because they would come early in the evening.

And when I think of that particular time, I remember beautiful smells in the house. Like Mum would be making either raisin bread or plum loaf, whatever you want to call it, and big, beautiful, thick molasses cookies—biscuits, they call them. Because she's going to serve a bit of lunch to all these people who are there.

We'd have so many people come, we wouldn't have enough chairs. My father would go out and bring in the big blocks of wood before it was split. And Mum would throw a cushion or an old jacket—whatever was around—on that. And the men would sit on that.

This is Christmas Eve, now, before church. I'd hear the sleighs coming in and the bells on the horses. It's a really, really nice memory that I have of all those people coming. It was exciting for us kids for all these people to come.

The Christmas of 1953

Marie Battiste

I will always remember the year I nearly lost my faith in Santa Claus. The year was 1953 and the Christmas season was coming on fast in the little town of Houlton, Maine. My mother and father were poorer than most, for few would hire "those Indians." My father and mother had to make baskets and sell them from door to door to make money for food and everything else we needed. Trying to sell enough for necessities was hard, but extra gifts at Christmas was even harder. It was less than a week away from Christmas and my parents had no money to buy food or toys for four children. But as the Christmas of 1953 turned out, it was to be the best Christmas of my life, though it didn't start out that way.

It was four days until Christmas and my mother, despite all her efforts, still had not sold a single basket. This meant to us that Christmas wasn't going to be very special this year. This wouldn't be the first Christmas that we couldn't buy toys or food. My mother told me of the time when I was three and my younger brother was just a newborn when Santa Claus first did not to come to our house. I was so young then that I didn't really understand what was happening. Now it was different; my younger sisters, Marie Ann and Gerry, were four and six and understood the practical side of the concept of Santa Claus.

This harsh reality of poverty was too hard for such young children to understand or accept, but my mother tried to explain it to my sister Gerry anyway. Marie Ann would have been happy with anything so our mother didn't want to tell her. Gerry, on the other hand, had seen a doll in the store window. It had a blue dress and a blue hat with matching coat and shoes. She fell in love with it the moment she saw it in the store window. For months all she talked about was this doll. Santa was all over the TV and often used to remind children to be good. She would ask Santa to bring it to her because she was a good girl as always. But now that we had no money, my mother knew it would be impossible to buy the doll for her. My mother tried to explain it to her. After much difficult thought, she decided she'd better warn her about the upcoming fate of her doll.

"Gerry, I need to tell you something. Santa's not bringing you the doll in the blue outfit this year," my mother said to her.

"Why not? I been a good girl," Gerry questioned.

"Gerry, you're a big girl now. There is no Santa Claus for big girls," our mother said quickly to Gerry as if it would make it hurt less.

"There is a Santa Claus I know it, I know there is one. There is. For me too. There is a Santa Claus. I saw him and he came last year. I know there is a Santa Claus for me. I know there is one," she said it in between her sobs. Gerry just sat and cried in her hands.

My mother then got up and walked into the bathroom, where she stayed until it was time to make supper. I don't think anyone knew this, but I heard her cry when she was in there. My younger sister Marie Ann asked me why Gerry was crying. I said she hurt her foot on the table.

It broke my heart to see my sister sit and cry at the table in the same state my mother left her in. I often wonder who it was harder on, Gerry or my mother.

I felt so bad that I turned to Tom and told him to collect the baskets in the sheet, because I was going to try to sell the baskets myself. He told me he would help tomorrow. I told him to keep it a secret from our mother.

The next day while everyone was still asleep, I tiptoed in my parents' room and quietly told my mother that Tom and I were going to try to sell the baskets. My mother agreed and wished us well. I didn't think she heard us as I went away. We then put on our winter jackets and collected two sheets full of baskets and went out into the cold winter morning.

We took our baskets to the nicest neighbourhood in town. Tall houses lined Court Street with big houses and front porches. By the time we got to the first house the snow began to fall. Soon it grew into a full-blown storm. The snow and wind blew all around us as we walked, covering our tracks as fast as we could walk. It was a cold and dark day, but our hope was too bright to be diminished by any storm. So we still went on, house to house inviting people to buy a basket.

Many people who answered the door invited us in, gave us something to eat and something hot to drink. I was so embarrassed every time one of my friends from school would open the door with puzzled looks. At almost every house there was either one of my friends or Tom's friends or classmates that answered the door. I was embarrassed with our poverty. But we needed to keep going. Each time we were led in and most of the time they bought one of our baskets, spreading open our sheet of baskets, looking them over and asking prices. Some wanted to buy the small ones, others wanted to buy the biggest one.

Sometimes when they would give us money and we didn't have change, they would say "Keep the change!" Even at one house, it was a two-dollar basket—Mom had priced them all beforehand so she would know how much they were—and they would give us five dollars. It was a great feeling on account of them being so generous to us and all. One by one the baskets were disappearing. By the time the light went behind the last house, we only had the wet dirty sheet left to drag home.

On our way home Tom, who was ten at the time, counted the money we got. I was really proud of myself for sticking to my goal to sell the baskets. I had what seemed like frozen feet and hands because I didn't have very warm mittens or boots. We got them from the church's secondhand clothing bin. It was hard to be poor in such cold weather.

As we walked up the stairs to our house, we could hear my father and mother's worried voices and questions about us. My father was mad because my mother let us go out in the storm. She didn't know it was going to storm.

We opened the door and looked in. Gerry was sitting on the couch with her long face, sniffing and wiping away tears quietly. Marie Ann was sitting beside her holding her hand and trying to comfort her. My parents looked up suddenly, relieved that we had finally got home. Then I told them about our day. The room went silent when Tom pulled out the wad of money which he counted on the way home. It was two hundred dollars, he announced, and told my parents of the people who we saw and what kind of food they gave us.

My father came over and picked me up and whispered in my ear how good of a daughter I was and how I saved Christmas for all of us. I think my mother was in a state of shock because she just stood there with her hands up to her face, covering her mouth, and with silent tears coming down. Both of them praised our journey and were amazed that we sold every single basket we took out. They made us explain how we got more money than we had baskets. They were so happy and excited about how much we made, the most money ever made in one trip. I never saw money like that until I grew up and got a job.

The next day my parents went to town. I babysat the children while they left. I tried to cheer up Gerry while they were gone because I knew my mother was probably in the department store as we sat, buying the doll in the blue dress for her. I wanted to tell her that everything was going to be great this Christmas and not to worry because Tom and I took care of it. She just sat on her bed and I wiped her nose. I told her just wait until tomorrow and find out the truth.

When my parents got home we had a feast of food, lots of candies and oranges. Tom and I got a special pie that our mother made when she got home, to celebrate our achievement. I remember that night my family sat and ate more food than we had eaten in a long time. It filled up our refrigerator with meat and good food—once again. Before there was just a bag of bread and mustard, but now it was so full we had to shut the door really hard to close it.

Christmas Day was the most memorable day of my life, it taught me that Santa Claus isn't an old man with a white beard. It taught me that Santa Claus was a spirit that looked over children all year and helped them have the best life that it could provide them with, considering the circumstances. That day Gerry got her doll with the blue dress, the one she dreamed about for weeks and was told she wouldn't get. When she unwrapped it, and pulled the doll out of the box, she marched right up to my mother, pointed at the doll.

"See, I told you there was a Santa Claus, I knew there was one and I was right. See everyone, there is a Santa Claus!" she said with tears in her eyes, but this time it was tears of joy.

The joy of Santa Claus never left her memory, even after she grew up and had kids of her own. She remembers how heartbroken she was and yet it turned out to be the best Christmas she ever had. I have never forgotten, either, that early December morning when I knew that someone was looking out for our family, making sure our spirits were bright on that special day. It was Santa Claus. That was the Christmas of 1953.

Old Santa Claus, 1918

Francis MacGregor

From April 1916 to November 1917 I served at the front, taking part in action at Ypres, the Somme, Vimy Ridge, Hill 70, and Passchendaele. This story has been told and retold by many. Only those who experienced the grim ordeal can know the roar of artillery, the bursting of shells, and the whine and whistle of machine and rifle bullets. The groans of the wounded and dying filled the scene with horror. About the last of November we took our final leave of Flanders. It was sad to leave many of the finest men I ever knew behind. But we were not sorry that we would never again see the mud of Belgium.

Old Santa Claus, 1918

About this time I was called into the Adjutant's tent and informed that I was one of the two from the 25th Battalion, due to long service in the line, to be sent home to Canada as an instructor in trench warfare. Seventy of us were picked from the various units. As large numbers of men were being conscripted, Canada asked that this should be done. I was stationed in Halifax. So after leave in London I sailed for Canada and after seventeen days at sea we arrived in Montreal. Once again we parted from old comrades and I went home on leave to Baddeck River before taking up my duties in Halifax.

My father met me in Baddeck with the old horse and buggy. He seemed very pleased and asked me what I intended to do and offered me the old home as he and my stepmother planned to move to Baddeck. I told him that I had to go back to Halifax and take on an easy job for a while.

When I got back to the old garrison city a few days after my leave had expired, the war was over. It was a wild day and night—November 11th, 1918. Now no more military duties. However, I did not get my discharge as my Battalion was on its way to Germany and they had my documents.

Coming home on leave for Christmas 1918, the train was crowded with service men. On getting into Truro it was still further overloaded with students from the Normal College and other passengers. Remember we were very happy, for this Christmas meant so much to those of us who had not enjoyed a Christmas during the war years.

At Truro an old man came aboard wearing whiskers and dressed in corduroys. It was impossible for him to find a seat in the already overcrowded train so, calling him "Santa Claus" and "Father Time," I took him through the train looking for a seat. My rank gave me enough authority to order some of the boys up in the smoking car to make room for him. A bottle of Scotch was passed around and he took a drink and joined in the general conversation without revealing his identity.

The train was hours late arriving at Iona. The ferry boat to Baddeck had gone back, leaving us stranded. The old gentleman mentioned that he had some heavy trunks in the baggage car and we volunteered to help him with them. The first big trunk that came out bore in large letters his name—Graham Bell. Two or three more trunks followed. It then dawned on us who he was and we felt that we should make some atonement for not showing him proper respect during the night on the train. Getting a platform lorry from the Station Master we proceeded to take his trunks to the wharf. He went into a little restaurant and called Beinn Bhreagh. A large motor boat came over and landed us all in Baddeck.

In about three weeks time a big reception was held in the Masonic Hall in Baddeck for those of us who had returned from Overseas. We found ourselves on the platform with the clergy and Alexander Graham Bell. He was asked to speak. He related his experiences saying how he enjoyed his trip in our company and quoted Burns:

> "For a' that and a' that, as comes it must for a' that,
> That man to man the world o'er, shall brothers be and a' that."

A Christmas Story

Jacques Côté

About six years after my father died from throat cancer in 1949 at age thirty-two, my mother started a "dime-dollar" store in my home town of 3500 people. No big box stores back then but still competition was swift. Just to distinguish her business from the others, my mom decided that I would dress up in a Santa Claus suit and post in front of the store after school to attract customers to the store during the two weeks before Christmas.

The suit she made me was made out of red cotton cloth and the trimming taken from a white rabbit fur coat that my sister wore as a very young child.

At first, I was pretty reluctant to do this but alas she convinced me to join in to keep the "bread earning" business afloat that was putting food on the table every day.

Much like today, an owner of a small family business needed to invest all its time, resources and sometimes health in the survival of the business. Christmas was no different for our store which was open from eight a.m. to ten p.m. every day for the four weeks before Christmas. Exceptionally closing at nine p.m. on Christmas Eve, needless to say that my mom had no energy left for the traditional midight celebrations at home.

One year, I think I was sixteen or seventeen, I had the crazy idea to show up in my Santa's suit at houses of people I knew who had younger children. After the Midnight Mass, my sister helped me put the accoutrement on and make up my face with rosy cheeks. As there was no snow on the ground, I jumped on my bike to do as many houses as I had planned before people would retire for a little bit of sleep by four to five a.m.

Big surprise at the first house . . . not as much an amazement for the parents as it was for me to see all the magic in the eyes of children thanking me, "Santa," personally, for the generosity, and making the promise to be good kids for the rest of the year . . . . As a good Santa, I had to leave in a hurry because I had lots of other young children to see. I devoured a piece of meat pie they gently offered me and left.

The night was absolutely wonderful. Not a single car on the road. Sky bright with zillions of stars shining. It was very moving. I showed up at several homes with all the same excitement; I even visited homes of seniors to bring them a few minutes of pure joy. I also stopped at houses of people I did not know well and everywhere it was thrill and fascination.

I still remember the last door I knocked at. A bunch of drunk adults pulled me in the house, offered me to share some of their hard stuff I never experienced before and did not want then. My interest was more to surprise the children and see the glint in their eyes. More with sadness than pride, they showed me their presents: a used pair of winter boots, old gloves, a torn-up truck, a puzzle and things like that. Each had a little bag of candies they had opened up but visibly not taken more than one. They wanted to share with me. . . . I could not take one.

That night Santa left that home very heartbroken. Taking a long detour, he biked back home pensive but blessed with his own good fortune.

A Little Christmas Joke

An older man in the Maritimes calls his son on the West Coast and says, "I hate to ruin your day, but I have to tell you that your mother and I are divorcing—thirty-five years of misery is enough."

"Dad, what are you talking about?" the son screams.

"We can't stand the sight of each other any longer," the older man says. "We're sick of each other, and I'm sick of talking about this, so you call your sister in Toronto and tell her"—and he hangs up.

Frantic, the son calls his sister, who explodes on the phone. "Like heck they're getting divorced," she shouts, "I'll take care of this."

She calls her father immediately, and she screams at him, "You are NOT getting divorced. Don't do a single thing until I get there. I'm calling my brother back, and we'll both be there tomorrow. Until then, don't do a thing, DO YOU HEAR ME?" —and hangs up.

The older man hangs up his phone and turns to his wife.

"Okay," he says, "they're coming for Christmas and paying their own fares. Now what do we tell them for next Christmas?"

"I am finally getting the Christmas spirit"

Verna Murphy

I am finally starting to get into the Christmas spirit. In a recent Facebook post, I asked about favourite Christmas treats. There were a lot of different replies, but it was my Aunt Lilly's answer that got me thinking.

Her favourites are Grandma's mincemeat and raisin pies. I had not thought of those for a few years and like my Aunt Lilly, I know my attempts at these treats just would not be the same as Grandma's. Just like I could not make Nanny's molasses cookies or rolls.

I remember asking her specifically about the cookies and rolls, but she always did a pinch of this, some of that and a lot of love—and never wrote down any of the recipes.

Once I started thinking about all the lost recipes, I thought I would share one of the best Christmas memories that I ever had in the hope that you will remember what the holidays should really be all about.

Picture it—rural Cape Breton, Christmas 1992. The old schoolhouse is lit up and neighbours and friends from Mabou Harbour can be seen sharing food, gifts and drink to start the holiday week. They gather outside to sing a few Christmas carols and light the tree as they do every year. But there is someone missing—and it is me.

I had a bone marrow transplant that fall of 1992 and I was told I might have to stay in Halifax over the holidays. After much begging and promises made to the doctors that I would follow all the rules, I found myself going home for Christmas, but due to the chance of infection I could not go to gatherings where there were many people.

So on the night of the Christmas party down the lane from my parents, I encouraged my family to go. There was no need of everyone missing out on all the fun just because I couldn't go.

I sat looking at the tree and thought how lucky I was to even be home, but I still had a pang of regret that I could not go to the party. And then there was a knock on the door and the first three people from the party arrived to wish me a Merry Christmas. After they left, another small group arrived and they kept coming the whole evening. They would leave the party and walk up my lane to come and wish me well. Many of them are gone now and others I have not seen for some years, but they gave me a magical night of feeling loved and I will treasure it always.

Whenever I am feeling overwhelmed with the pressures of shopping, cleaning and baking during the holidays I sit down in front of the tree—whenever I get it up—and I think of that night all those years ago and how such a simple gesture by so many gave me a wonderful gift. And for the last nineteen years it made me remember what is most important when our lives get so crazy busy. Love, kindness and simple acts of generosity are the things that are remembered, not the gifts that are given.

My science teacher, Edmund Cummings, was filling in for Santa that night and he came to hear what I wanted for Christmas. Someone snapped a picture of the two of us that night and it was the only picture I allowed anyone to take while I was sick—there I was with no hair or eyebrows, my eyes are swollen and so are my cheeks. And I have the biggest grin on that I have ever seen on myself in a picture. I had found the joy that we all search for during the holidays and I can still take it out and remember it whenever I want.

Christmas in the Coal Mine—An Initiation

Jim MacLellan
of The Men of the Deeps

Years ago, miners had to work on Christmas Eve. We'd only work on Christmas Day in the case of an emergency, such as a fire, flood, an explosion, electrical or mechanical breakdown, or even a bad roof fall. Any one of which could result in a brother miner being either badly hurt, or even killed. It would take a very serious incident to keep a miner from his family on Christmas Day.

I'd like to tell you a true story that happened to me, many years ago on Christmas Eve.

In 1954 at age twenty I was transferred from Caledonia Colliery, where I had worked for the previous three years, to Number 20 Colliery.

Now Caledonia was a very old colliery, with horses pulling the boxes that the men loaded coal and stone into with great big pan shovels. Whereas Number 20 was a modern, mechanized mine, using 125-horsepower locomotives to haul men, coal, and materials in and out. And the locomotives were equipped with radios whose receivers could be heard for great distances throughout the mine. Number 20 also had fully mechanized advance-and-retreat longwall faces, with the coal being won by Dosco Continuous Miners.

The coal in Caledonia was only about five feet high, where the levels in Number 20 were up as high as ten feet. That was quite a change for me.

My story begins late in seven-to-three shift on Christmas Eve. We were sitting in the rakes up on the North Landing and patiently waiting for the trip to start out. Now a rake is a wooden box designed to hold ten men, five on each side, sitting facing one another. And a rake trip consists of ten boxes, or one hundred men.

Also, I was the oldest of a very large family. And my mother was expecting me to pick up the toys that she had on layaway at the Lipkus toy store. And also I had to get a gift for my girlfriend Elsie, whom I later married. So you can see I was rather anxious to get going.

So finally, finally, the trip started out. And I was oh so relieved, you know. But after we got out maybe a thousand feet, it suddenly came to a stop. And I said, "Oh my gosh, I'm never going to get home!" So I stand up in the rake and I'm shining my light around and I'm being rather obnoxious, you know.

An older miner was sitting across from me and he reached over and he got me by the coat and he give it a tug. In a stern voice he said, "Siddown! Shut up! And put out your light!"

When an older miner spoke, you listened.

So I sat down and I put out my light and I huddled up in my coat. As I looked around, everybody had their lights out. We were in total darkness. It was very eerie and deadly quiet. The only sound was the hum of the cold, frigid air whipping by my face. And then suddenly from the dispatcher's radio I heard him say, "They're all stopped there." Gosh—that meant that the other two rakes were stopped also. I said to myself, "Three rakes, stopped in this cold, cold motor road. What's going on?"

Then, as if by cue, a lyrical tenor voice sailed across the airwaves, singing "Silent Night, Holy Night." I couldn't believe it! There we were, three hundred coal miners, huddled together on this cold, damp roadway, five miles out and three thousand feet down under the Atlantic Ocean, listening to this famous hymn, on Christmas Eve!

It was so beautiful. I felt a chill go up my back, and goose bumps start breaking out all over me. I was totally overwhelmed. This was a Christmas Eve I'd not soon forget.

Just as that voice finished singing his hymn, the older miner who had scolded me earlier leaned across and with a smile said, "Merry Christmas, Son!" And I didn't know what to say, so with a choked voice I said, "S-s-same to you, sir!"

And then as we were starting out, the voice of the dispatcher boomed across the airwaves saying, "Merry Christmas to all! And to all, have a good night!"

The Christmas Concert

Elsie Aucoin Frontain

The Christmas concert was a major event in the country school. Our school served both the English-speaking and Acadian French populations. We were a happy mix in a two-room school. Shortly after Halloween—which was not a big thing in my early years except that we drew pictures of black witches on brooms, black cats and bats and stuck them on the window panes with home-made glue—the teachers in the neighbouring districts collaborated as to the dates of the concert, materials to be shared, curtains to be borrowed, sometimes a Santa suit, etc.

Nellie à Benie Leblanc was a long-time teacher in Margaree East and her Christmas concerts were of a high calibre. The hall in that community was large with a good stage and proper curtains. They also owned a red Santa suit, trimmed with white, a wide black shiny belt, and a beard that didn't fall off if the elastic became loose. In an age of limited communication except by letter or meeting before church, I am amazed at how well these plans materialized.

In our school, the primary grades (*le p'tit boutte*) and the senior grades (*le gran boutte*) each had their programs, practised individually, and as the concert date approached, got together for a combined practice or two.

The primary classes, Grades 1 to 4, (in my day) were chosen to do the Address of Welcome, some folk dances, a recitation or two, and a couple of carols. The French/English Catholic children sang "Angels We Have Heard on High" or a French one "Il Est Né Le Divin Enfant." The Protestant children always sang "Away In a Manger"—the best! We didn't know what "Gloria in Excelsius Deo" meant—it was Latin.

The folk dances involved four couples, distinct patterns (movements) and music. Albert à Arsène Chiasson from the *gran boutte* played the mouth organ and was happy to use his talent. His tunes were from the Don Messer weekly radio program, two of which I remember, "The Little Burnt Potato" and "The Stack of Barley." The rhythm and the beat were right for the dance.

We wrote our own lines—copied from the blackboard—and memorized our parts and the songs. Practice started at the end of November but seriously by December 10th or so.

Lorette LeBlanc Miller couldn't sing but she was a great director so she put us through our paces and we bowed, skipped, wove in and out, and swung our partner in the small space allowed by pushing back the seats. We didn't know then that we were as good as the Austrian children in *The Sound of Music*.

Finally we joined the big room (*le gran boutte*) for combined practice. It was amazing to see the "seniors" dressed in unusual clothing for the pageant. Outfits of homemade costumes, bath robes, towels wrapped around their heads, odds and ends of belts and veils to resemble the Middle Eastern people as seen on Holy Cards and Bible pictures. The stage at the K.I.W. Hall—Knowledge Is Wealth, as named by a past educator, John J. LeBlanc—was too small to accommodate animals, real or fake, so they were left out of the Holy Scene.

The Holy Birth narrative from the Gospel of Saint Luke was my first proclamation of Scripture and I still remember the feeling of it. We prayed for fine weather. There could be nothing worse than a snowstorm to change the plans, and it sometimes happened.

We exchanged names and were to give a present to the one we had picked. It was supposed to be kept secret but usually word got out. Suggestions for gifts were given. Boys liked *un couteau d'poche* (pen knife), a toy airplane kit or a new pair of laces for their gumshoes. Girls were easier to find gifts for—perfume, soaps that smelled good, barrettes for hair, and fancy writing paper for the teacher. The catalogues, Eatons and Simpsons, were the sources of Christmas shopping, and when the parcel came we were often disappointed with a "not in stock" pink slip or a substitute article which just didn't fit. Many times we resorted to the local store, Léo à Mose Chiasson, for a scribbler and a pencil. Knitted items of home-grown woollen yarns were not as well received as store-bought ones.

Our mothers contributed their patience and other talents, especially sewing outfits and making brown sugar fudge. This was brown-bagged (small) and sold at the concert to help with expenses. The profits were small! Ten cents a bag.

The cutting of the Christmas tree was a major event which had to be planned close to the concert date. Since it was a fresh tree and kept indoors (without water) it had to be cut the day before. The "boys," about seven or so of them, convinced the teacher that there was "safety in numbers," "many hands make light work," etc., so off to the woods they went to the *parc à vache à Saira* (Sarah) or deeper woods to search for the right tree, not

41

too big, and a fir, because the spruce dropped its needles. There were lots more spruce than fir! A stop at Tante Yanne's store (Miss Flora Gallant) or Willie D. Matheson's fortified their supply of cigarettes (or makings and Chantecler papers if you rolled your own); if other supplies were purchased they remained unnamed. They eventually returned, dragging the semblance of a Christmas tree and set it up near the stage in a corner, where the girls later decorated it with items brought from home. The hall had electricity but the small lights so popular and accessible today had not yet reached Belle Côte.

Fir boughs with red crepe paper bows were hung at the windows, adding a festive look to the otherwise drab appearance of the building. The smell of fresh fir was also welcome. The windows, lacking blinds, were often covered with black tar paper to keep out the light.

The night of the concert was an exciting one. We were scrubbed clean, shampooed and dressed in our best. One year I was in the folk dance for which the girls were required to wear a white dress. I hadn't owned or worn one since my First Communion. This meant I had to borrow one. It didn't quite fit me but I had no choice. I wore it anyway and since there were no change rooms at the hall I had to wear it all through the concert in lieu of the pretty plaid dress my sister had sent me from Boston!

My brother Wilfred (now ninety-five years old) fared even worse. His teacher, Theresa à Eddie à Lubin Leblanc, had him dress as a plum pudding! What could he wear to make himself look like a plum pudding? "I wore a potato sack. I think it was stuffed with old newspapers. We didn't have much to work with so we had to use our imagination and invent something." More probably our mother's imagination. We can picture him arriving home with the news he had been chosen for a part in the concert and Lucie Anne immediately assuming he was to be Joseph, or at the very least one of the shepherds. Then to learn his part was that of a plum pudding must have left her speechless for a few moments.

Such a dessert was not part of an Acadian mother's recipe book, which featured tapioca, bread puddings, and vanilla puddings, so she must have consulted her Scotch neighbour Jessie Munro for a description of a plum pudding so as to create a costume for her son. In any event, Wilfred appeared in the concert looking like a pudding or a stuffed potato sack. Wilfred adds, "I had a stand-in, in case I took an asthma attack inside the sack. I think it was Henri à Severin à Pekin or perhaps Mose à John Joe. They lived in the 'Concession,' (the backlands) and came to school through the woods."

The "big boys" were in charge of operations. This included the curtains, which were a challenge at best, the props (they were sparse), making the announcements, and helping to keep all other comments to whispers—"Where's the rabbit wire?"

Everyone came to the event, even parents who no longer had children in school. Where else could you go to be so well entertained for twenty-five cents? They came on foot, in horse and sleigh (*en traine à bois*), and in a few trucks.

The schoolchildren and others involved could put their coats, boots and stuff upstairs, but the general audience kept their coats on and sat on long benches across the room (clearing the stove) and along the side walls.

The program lasted about two hours, with the closing farewell recitation followed by—what else? Here comes Santa Claus!

A commotion is happening at the door—sleigh bells are jangling and there he is, the red-suited man with a sack on his back, calling out "Ho Ho Ho!" making his way up to the stage near the tree, where he speaks to the children, calling their names as he recognizes the neighbourhood children and begins to hand out goodies in bags and the exchange gifts as well. He had lots of assistants teasing them all the while. Of course, we knew who was wearing the red suit; who else could stepdance like that?

During the war ('39–'45) we missed some of the talent as entertainers. Pierre à Anselme LeLievre (RCN) was the right size for Santa and with some liquid refreshment beforehand had been very entertaining. Paddé à Johnnie Delaney (the stepdancer) was a great stand-in, never stuck for a word, quips, and the odd personal comment for certain parents, teachers and all. Such fun! Wilbert à Joe played a mean fiddle when he was available.

Long after the event was over, the lines and songs we had learned and memorized remained in our memory. We discovered gifts and talents we had not realized we had. We were taught how to bow and to curtsy, please and thank you, to enunciate difficult words even if missing some front teeth. We came to know and to appreciate our teachers who had been our directors. They had given us a new view of ourselves, a new confidence in facing an audience while being applauded by those who were proud of us.

The $25,000 Acadian Meat Pie and *Le Réveillon*

Rosie Aucoin Grace

Eating meat pies has long been an important part of an Acadian tradition referred to as *Réveillon*, a word the dictionary translates as "Christmas Eve or New Year's Eve dinner," or simply "to celebrate Christmas or New Year's Eve."

Recently, there was much excitement and a deep sense of pride among people of the Acadian region of Inverness County as they received the news that Alcide (Al) Desveaux had won the Savoury Pie Challenge on CBC-TV's *Recipe to Riches* with his family recipe for Acadian Meat Pies that for merchandising purposes he calls "Grandpa's Acadian Meat Pie"—even though, it must be pointed out, Alcide credits his success to the crust which comes from a recipe passed down from an aunt in Cape Breton. Alcide's recipe earned him a spot on *Recipe to Riches* where he was up against other top amateur Canadian cooks. The judges were instantly struck by the delicious taste of Alcide's dish. And after successfully competing in cooking and marketing challenges, Alcide's savoury pie made him the episode finalist. The very next day, the *Steven and Chris Show* featured Alcide as a guest and, since then, Alcide's schedule has been filled to the brim! What incredible overnight exposure!

According to Alcide, who now lives in Welland, Ontario, in the old days Acadians used wild game. Today he uses shredded pork and chicken with a touch of onion and a mix of salt, pepper and summer savoury.

"Just about everybody in the Chéticamp area makes their own style, and mine, why it would be special? I don't know. My crust seems to be a big secret. A lot of people like the crust. The type of meat I use is the dark meat of the chicken and the fairly fat part of the pork and it makes a very juicy pie you can easily eat cold."

Alcide likes to end up with a thick crust and uses a double-aluminum plate with the bottom painted black. That way, the plate absorbs the heat and firmly cooks the bottom crust.

Seventy-four-year-old Chef Alcide, son of Alex à Philippe à Arsène Desveaux and Rita à Didier Delaney, was born and raised in beautiful Cap LeMoine, Cape Breton. Although he grew up with wonderful home-cooked Acadian meals, serious cooking for him only started later on in life, but he found that it came naturally. His love for cooking always close to his heart, he even opened a large Bridge Club with about thirty-five tables, and also ran a small restaurant where he served Acadian meals such as blood pudding, head cheese and, of course, meat pies.

"My clientele loved the food and we had good times! I cook like in the old days. I do not follow a set recipe but rather a little bit of this and that, to taste."

And regarding winning $25,000 in a meat pie contest? "It is incredible. . . . *Incroyable!* To tell you the truth, I am exhausted. I am on the phone from early morning to evening with countless interviews and some appearances, but it's all good! The hardest part was to keep this a secret from everyone except my wife since last August. The two of us could not tell a soul. Now, that was hard. I am so relieved that the show has now been aired and that it is finally out there!

"It was not easy competing on national television. I was somewhat nervous and at times a bit overwhelmed. Like when I had to make one hundred meat pies in three hours. Whew!"

During the show, as part of the marketing competition, Alcide needed to get people to taste and love his product. Viewers saw him on a beach in Toronto, dressed up like a lumberjack, accompanied by a fiddler and approaching strangers, enticing them to come taste his product. It was a hit! Later on in the show, one of the judges asked Alcide if people tasting the product mentioned if there should be more spices added and Alcide answered, "On the contrary, they seem to love the simplicity of the meat pies."

Full of passion and with much emotion, Alcide spoke from the heart: "Imagine all across Canada, sharing my recipe which is a part of my heritage. It is so exciting! After we watched the show on Wednesday night, the phone calls from home in Cape Breton, all the e-mails, messages on Facebook, it has been amazing! My family and friends have been so supportive in all this." He added, "To think this all started with my love for *La Cuisine.* My family loves this Acadian specialty. Every Christmas, Lise and I go to Sarnia and we make meat pies for them."

Of course, Alcide Desveaux's good fortune brings me back to the meaning of Christmas and the place of meat pies in Acadian traditions, to its central place in Cape Breton—*Le Réveillon,* the meal after Midnight Mass. I can't help but remember stories told by our ancestors. One visit in particular is a story told to me by the late Marie-Hélène à Émilien à Marcellin Chiasson of Saint-Joseph-du-Moine who was married to Joseph à William Doucet, in Marie-Hélène and Joseph's cabin. It was a good interview but it got even better when we started talking about Christmas. Marie-Hélène brightened up and spoke with pride and joy of her childhood Christmases with her family.

"We were brought up in the family where we all loved one another. We were very close and loved to do special things to make others happy.

"Christmas was such an exciting time. It all started with the killing of a cow or pig. We had no refrigerators then so we had to store the meat in wooden boxes under the snow. Now, we can make and freeze meat pies year round. We couldn't do that back then.

"We had a big table in the dining room and during Christmas time, my mother would make meat pies and bake goodies for us. Nothing fancy like today, just gingerbread, molasses or sugar cookies. They were some good and would be all gone the very same day!"

I asked Marie-Hélène about their decorations. "Ah, the decorations were rare. Dad and my brothers would go out and cut down a tree. We'd make our own decorations using candles and the bottoms of cans to hold the candles on the tree. Sometimes, we made flowers out of crepe paper. I'd be curious to see those decorations again. I know now we can buy beautiful ornaments but those were special because we made them together as a family. It was so much fun!"

After more description of these wonderful decorations, we moved on to the presents. Marie-Hélène said, "Oh God, we never got anything costly, more like a few treats. Our mother was kind and very wise. She would tell us that if we helped out with the chores, she'd make us something fancy, like a small apron. It was just her way of encouraging us to continue with the house chores. We'd get some candies and maybe some fruit, nothing extravagant, that's all there was, but we were so excited just the same. We couldn't wait to eat those juicy oranges and apples!"

She continued, "A very special part of our Christmas celebration was all the visitors. Our house was a place where many people gathered known as *La maison du monde*. They'd come from near and far and everyone was in such good cheer!"

And about Christmas Eve: "Midnight Mass was so special, you couldn't wait to go! At that time, we were very excited about the birth of baby Jesus and also waited anxiously for a visit from Père Noël. In our family, faith played a very important role in our lives, especially so at Christmas time.

"In those days, Midnight Mass was the only Mass that took place at night so it was quite exciting. My God, the Christmas hymns were beautiful! Even today, when I hear those songs, it brings me right back to my childhood days. Coming home from Midnight Mass, some people would sing Christmas carols and others rushed home in anticipation for the *réveillon*, the feast of meat pies and goodies waiting at home. It was such a magical night, you could see the lanterns swaying in the air as the horse and sleighs went by, it was so touching. We could see them coming down Bazile Road on to the lake, you know Le Lac à Dosite, and then right past our house. There was always lots of snow and the lake was frozen. It was a beautiful sight, lanterns raised while the sound of people singing and the sleigh bells ringing filled the air!"

A Child's Christmas Day Diary, 1914

Ella Liscombe

For Christmas I got a book called *Tanglewood Tales* and a Chatterbox, two games called Old Maid and Pit and the stuff and pattern to make a pair of bloomers, leggings from Ollie. From Papa and Mamma I got a pair of hockey skates and boots and from Lewis a scribbler and from Trixie three handkerchiefs. From Aunt Emily and Uncle Fred I got a book, handkerchief and necklace.

On Christmas Day we had a great big turkey we nicknamed the "Kaiser" (I wish the Kaiser is as dead as he is now) we had grandma and grandpa to dinner.

Christmas in the First World War

Fr. Leo Sears

We got orders to return to Vimy, to the Ridge, to prepare for the Germans' last effort, which was very nearly successful. On the way out, we spent our Christmas—oh Lord, I've forgotten the name of the place—but we were billeted in a hay mow with chickens over our head, on the side of a canal. But our Christmas parcels had all come through, and we had a marvellous Christmas dinner, with lots of refreshments.

(*Would you have clergy with you?*) No, we went to the church in the French village, half-ruined church, with daylight showing through the rafters. One of the Christmases I'll always remember. It was an old French priest, not a young one, who had the Midnight Mass. Only old people there. And girls, and children. Christmas Day, in the evening, we were on the side of a canal—some way or other, some of the lads found bicycles in the village, and very happy, they started riding up and down the canal.

(*Religion had not left you?*) It was very important. While we were waiting to get ready to go into our final position for the attack on Passchendaele, it was brought to our attention that there would be a Catholic chaplain at Ypres on a certain day.

We got permission to go into Ypres this day, to get to confession. And we went there in the morning. We stayed there all day. There were crowds of Canadian soldiers, Canadian Catholics, waiting their turn to go to confession. And late that evening, the chaplain came out, and he said, "I'm sorry. I've been hearing all day, and I can hardly hear any longer. I'm dead beat." He gave us general absolution, which was a comfort, going into the line.

You've often heard that expression that there are no atheists in a shellhole. It's perfectly true. It makes a difference. Anybody who had ever had any faith, experienced a revival of faith. (*I would think of war as such a hardener.*) It hardened, and it softened. It hardened to the experience of violence. It softened you to the extent of wondering how God could allow this violence to occur, and that the reason must be rebellion of man against God—that God would leave mankind to find his way out of the situation for which he was responsible himself.

And of course, the sense of camaraderie and loyalty to one's friends was out of this world. Especially in an outfit that was small enough where everybody knew everybody else. I was lucky in that respect. You see, the infantry, where casualties were so frequent, where replacements were so numerous, you were never sure of how long you would be with your friends. Although, after Vimy, the McGill outfit got reinforcements. They were all lumberjacks from Nova Scotia and New Brunswick. And I remember, when we heard who were coming, I remember saying, "Are we going to have two camps in this outfit when those boys arrive?" Ten days after they arrived, you wouldn't know which were the students and which were the lumberjacks.

Ukrainian Christmas Celebrations

Fr. Roman Dusanowskyj

In late October, early November, all the stores set out their Christmas decorations, play Christmas music and invite the public to join in the Christmas spirit. There is laughter and singing, toys and gifts. Everyone wishing all "a Merry Christmas." This celebration and feasting continues until December 25th. The next day, the day after Christmas, Christmas lights are turned off, all decorations are taken down and not a carol to be heard. The traditional twelve days of Christmas are lost and forgotten. But not by all. For some, as in the Ukrainian community in Sydney, Christmas Day is not the end of celebrations, but the beginning—and not once, but twice.

The Sydney community is unique in that it celebrates Christmas twice. On December 25th and then again on January 7th. We do not celebrate the twelve days of Christmas—we celebrate the twenty-four days of Christmas!

The December 25th celebration is for family. That is the time of year when children are off school, many people take time off work so that family can celebrate together.

But why January 7th? January 7th on everyone's wall calendar is December 25th on the Julian Calendar. Currently, the Julian Calendar lags 13 days behind the Gregorian calendar and it loses 1 day every 100 years. So in the year 2100, Christmas on the Julian calendar will fall on January 8th. The Julian Calendar is still followed Liturgically by the Eastern Slavic Churches (Russian, Ukrainian and Bielorussian) and is used by the Greek church to calculate Easter.

Christmas Eve is a very holy evening and the highlight of Christmas celebrations. It has nothing to do with gift giving. All gifts have been given on the feast of St. Nicholas on December 6th (December 19th on the Julian Calendar). It is all about the celebration of the birth of Christ.

By tradition, straw is placed on the floor of the dining area and hay is placed under the tablecloth, both symbolizing the stable and the manger. A sheath of wheat is placed in the corner of the room, each kernel representing a deceased member of the family (the ancestors).

An extra chair and plate is placed at the table (often with a burning candle on the plate). Its purpose is two-fold. Firstly, it is the place where the ancestors may join in the meal. A small portion of every course is placed on the plate. Secondly, if a stranger should come knocking at the door, it is a place at the table ready to receive him or her. Christmas Eve is a night when no one is turned away and no one should go hungry.

The Holy Meal begins with the appearance of the first star. It is a twelve-course meal, both meatless and dairyless. The elder of the family offers each person a piece of bread (*prosfora*) with honey and greets them with the words "Christ is born!" The person receiving the bread responds with "Glorify Him!"

The first course is *kutia*—a cold mixture of cooked wheat,

honey and crushed poppy seeds (some add nuts and raisins), again representing the deceased. Christmas Eve is an evening where the living and the dead join together to celebrate and welcome the birth of our Lord God and Saviour, Jesus Christ. This is followed by borscht (beet soup), pyrogies, cabbage rolls, beans, mushrooms, etc. (all meatless and dairyless). It is the responsibility of the children to count the courses to make sure that there are twelve courses served. As each course is brought to the table, a carol is sung. If there are small children present, candy and chocolates are scattered in the straw and the children enjoy a treasure hunt at the end of the meal.

After the meal all go to church. Christmas Services begin late on Christmas Eve with Great Complines ("Complines" means the service after supper) which concludes with the blessing of bread, wine, wheat and oil. The theme of the service is "God is with us." This is followed by the Divine Liturgy, with much enthusiasm, much joy and happiness—and of course, much caroling.

The greeting of the season is "Christ is born!!" and the response is "Glorify Him!!"

The Christmas season lasts for twelve days and finishes on the Eve of Theophany. During this period, it is the tradition to go and visit people with carol singing and well-wishing.

January 7th celebrations are for celebrating Christmas with our brothers and sisters in Ukraine. For many years it was forbidden to celebrate Christmas in Ukraine (or any religious holiday), punishable by many years in prison. The people of Ukraine counted on us to celebrate Christmas for them. Today, they are free to celebrate Christmas and every other holiday. But for the Ukrainian community in Sydney it has become a tradition that we are only too happy to continue.

CHRIST IS BORN !!!!   GLORIFY HIM !!!

Remembering D.W. MacLeod

Frank and Margaret MacRae

The only story that I know, that D.W. told, the time he was out trapping out in the woods, during winter. He came home. And he was telling the story. And they were talking about how cold it was last night. Oh, he said, it was terrible cold where he was last night: that the light in the lamp froze! The kerosene lamp, you know—that it was so cold that the flame froze.

Margaret MacRae: He was great at telling stories like that, you know, just to be funny, and people used to get a kick out of them.

He used to make up these stories—they were just lies, you know. He used to make them up for fun, just to entertain people. He loved to entertain them. People who would gather like that in a house in the evening. D.W. was there—that would be the entertainment for the evening, D.W. telling stories that he made up.

He was telling one time about the bear, when he got him on the pole of the wagon. He was hauling supplies out to the Oregon—a pulp-cutting operation at St. Ann's—when the Oregon was working. And he was going out with a load, a big wagon full of supplies. And he was on his way out, halfways up the mountain—here he met this big bear ahead of him on the road. And oh, he didn't know what he was going to do.

The bear stood his ground. He didn't know what he was going to do. He didn't have a gun or anything. But he had a cask of molasses on the load, along with the other supplies. So he took the horses out of the wagon—the wagon had a pole between the two horses, you know—and he tied them to the back of the wagon. And he knocked the bung out of the keg of molasses and he smeared the pole with molasses. The bear started licking the pole and eating the pole. And as he was going along, the pole was going down his throat. Finally the pole came out on the other end. And he put the pin in it, and he had it—the bear tied to the pole! Well, people would listen to that and laugh to kill themselves!

Frank: Oh, he was great to pass time, you know. *Margaret*: He lived out in West Tarbot. D.W.'d come in and he'd sit and tell stories. He was as happy as a lark—there was nobody happier than he was. Anywhere. He raised his family, and they grew up, and they survived.

I often tell the little story about—he used to be Santa Claus quite often. Whenever there'd be a Christmas concert in the schoolhouse over here or at Tarbot, D.W. would be the Santa Claus. He was the right build, I guess. He was good at doing that sort of thing, make a good Santa Claus. They'd dress him up and he'd have the fur coat on, and the mask and the whole bit.

His own little girls—one year at Christmas time the girls were there at the concert, and they were sitting in a row in the front seat, waiting expectantly for Santa Claus to come. Santa Claus came in and he started giving out the gifts and saying little things to the children. And they were looking at him pretty close. They must have—they guessed who it was. I think they recognized his shoes.

And they'd say one to the other, "'S e brogan Daddy a th'ann." ("He's got Daddy's shoes on.") One would say to the other, "'S e brogan Daddy a th'ann." They were disputing among themselves. And then he'd say, "Oh," he would say, "I have to hurry up. Feumaidh mi falbh gun a' North Pole." ("I have to go to the North Pole.") "Cha teid cas dhiot gun a' North Pole," ("Not a foot of you will go to the North Pole,") the little girls would say. "We're not going to the North Pole tonight, whoever is going!" Oh well, people were getting such a kick out of the little ones.

A Jewish Child's Christmas in Cape Breton

Joseph Sherman

Butch and Gordie and I left the old car by the side of the road in Sydney River. One hatchet between us, we moved slowly into the near woods, disregarding any timber lifting higher than about nine feet. What they were searching for, what I was searching for in their name, had to be tall but not too tall, fat and full but not too fat and full. I set upon one young tree with a future. They had choices of their own. Mine came down first, sweeping to earth almost noiselessly, bringing with it burning flakes of the day's fresh snow set adrift from the branches of tree fallen and trees disturbed. Otherwise, the late-December air was absolutely clear.

My perfect tree metamorphosed after being felled. It was now significantly bare on one side, and much too long as it lay like an intrusion across the white of the forest floor. More sounds, more snow, and a second tree came down. Gordie's blade bit new wood again and again, and I finally began to feel the cold. We all of us stomped and hissed at our own breath and left with the last to fall because it was getting late, the light beginning to make newer shadows of everything upright.

Less than a week till Christmas. With the balding, bowed tip jutting from the rear window of the green Henry J, and with road snow flying upward through the rents in its floorboards, we drove back into Sydney and Whitney Pier. I passed on the decorating and went home to my supper. After all, it wasn't my tree.

There is no Jewish Christmas, and therefore no Jewish Santa Claus. Any celebrating I might do is unsanctioned and entirely of my own volition. Some gentiles think that Chanukah and Passover are the Jewish equivalents of Christmas and Easter, probably because the holidays do cyclically pair up in proximity to each other. I am convinced, however, that the majority of Christians refuse to consider the possible existence of any sort of religious holiday that does not, in some way, include what they themselves purport to celebrate. A religious event taking place in December must surely honour the birth of Christ, one in April must be inspirited by the Resurrection.

After years of this I am tempted to holster my old denials and decree a moratorium—declare a festival of lights to be a festival of lights.

Though I have never fully observed the rites of Christmas, my personal involvement has often extended beyond the peripheral. Besides, the most colourful and exciting aspects of the holiday are, as I learned later than some, pagan in origin. Christmas was largely a vicarious thrill for me throughout my 1950s childhood in Whitney Pier, though my mother has bought and stuffed a turkey for dinner on the twenty-fifth for as long as I can remember, and there's nothing Jewish about that.

On that day I would invariably dash across Wesley Street fairly early in the morning, so as to be in time for at least the last of my best friend's family gift opening. I would gladly lend a hand at breaking in the new toys and games. After, I would seek out the loaded bowls of nuts and head home with my pockets knuckled like squirrel's cheeks.

At an earlier age yet, I had been made aware of the reasons preventing me from having a tree of my own, but I was never prevented from choosing to be a sort of collaborator. Past the mezuzah waymarks of my then-kosher home, I made up for many losses incurred as a non-Christian.

My first three remembered Christmases were experienced in the home of a Ukrainian neighbour when I was barely old enough to cross unpaved Muggah Street alone. Late December in that household brought me the aromas of an exotic world. The greenness of their ceiling-high tree soared through a webbing of coloured lights, multi-hued tinsel balls and icicles, and the white froth of sticky angel hair which I was always invited to toss. This was years before Sydney River and the Henry J. I was most entranced by the candle-shaped lights with their bubble effect, which, when the parlour lights were switched off, would hold my eyes for an evening of hours.

The family had a vintage Victrola to wind and play, the older Dilney girls bestowed smiles I was keen to receive, and the snow-drifts lay safely beyond the thick-wintered windows.

Just prior to Christmas vacation, elementary and junior high school used to be subject to a contagion of celebrants; the class-rooms were decorated with dwarf trees and cut-outs, and smelly, Gestetnered sheaves of carols were distributed to each pupil. Every teacher had this once-a-year opportunity to lead a not always inspired songfest, and in the brief lull between numbers sung in one class you could hear another roomful of voices issuing from the opposite end of the hall. Somewhere between and through these renditions ran others from other rooms, ensuring that Whitney School was anything but tranquil in that time leading up to the holidays.

On the last day of school, the teachers would form a procession and sing their way upstairs and down, two by two, in through one classroom door and out the other, grown-up laughter and uncoordinated music mingling with the kids' derisive comments. In my final year there I remember watching Mrs. Crouse, my Grade Eight teacher, and Mr. MacIsaac, my Grade Nine manual training instructor, go skippng along, arm in arm, near the head of the line—one galumphing coal car behind the huffing red engine of Santa, stout and compact, baggy but utterly sincere— our principal.

I wasn't supposed to sing Christmas carols, and I resented being seduced by the spirit of the occasion, just as I used to resent the efforts of an earlier teacher of mine to get me to sing morning hymns with the rest of my class. She would tell me that it could do no harm if I sang "Jesus Loves Me" and "God Sees the Little Sparrow Fall." I did waver over the Christless "Rock of Ages" but remained adamant in my refusal to join in wholeheartedly. Where the carols were concerned, I timorously sang along with as many as I could permit myself—so many of the tunes having become familiar and appealing to me over the years—leaving blanks where the name of Christ appeared (though some of my more defiant Jewish friends would occasionally substitute a distinctly inappropriate word). One year, much to my embarrassment, I heard my own voice taking the lead on "Good King Wenceslas."

The only Christmas gifts I ever gave were in school, but I was not the first in my family to behave generously on such a transparently non-Jewish occasion. My maternal grandmother, a Jewish matriarch like no other, found good reason of her own for gift-giving. In Bridgewater, the small town where she and my grandfather ran a family clothing store, she found herself moved to action by the economic plight of some of her fellow townsfolk, though her own family was far from affluent. Each Christmas, until the year she died, she arranged with her grocer to have baskets delivered to several families in need. These were filled, not with perishables that wouldn't see a second day, but with practical stuff such as boxed and canned goods, flour and meal, that would provide sustenance well past the holidays. Hers was an anonymous gesture, and it was only after my grandmother's death that the grocer would acknowledge her actions to those who might have suspected, all along, just who their benefactor had been.

In elementary school it was the practice to have us draw names in early December, with each child expected to give a small gift to the classmate whose name had been selected, no exceptions allowed. The gifts were to be brought to class on the last day before Christmas vacation, and it was always exciting, almost voyeuristic, to discover what each classmate's mother had thought appropriate. My own mother generally gift-wrapped a shiny pencil box, a bow tie, an undershirt or a jigsaw puzzle. Each year I would long to have my name drawn by one of the girls, and to draw a girl's name myself, but it never happened.

I recall the year I had to go partners with John Pilsudski, an unwashed nuisance who would go out of his way to aggravate me through my first nine years of school. In high school I was to fall briefly in love with his sister, but back in that particular year of gift-exchanges through systemic coercion, I was determined to see that John received something as meaningful as rat poison or roach killer. My mother insisted on a necktie.

That last December school day saw the classroom strewn with white tissue paper and a blizzard of Christmas seals. My offering was dispersed with the rest, and then I received my own reward, a flat, thinly wrapped item which I ripped open while my nemesis was still wrestling with the generous folds of paper around his clip-on necktie. I've never hated more intensely, nor felt more significantly out of place at any gentile gathering, than I did on that day when I was forced to show everyone what I'd been given: no new game or pencil box but an orange, unruled scribbler worth a flat nickel. I don't believe that I've ever forgiven either of us for that day, that Christmas.

The year I took part in my only Christmas pageant I was in Grade Five, the sole Jewish child in class. I was given the role of the lead Wise Man, who came to worship at the manger with his two sage companions, and who was the only one with anything to say. Though a part of me was intoxicated at taking the little stage, I felt exposed and uncomfortable in my new skin. But I had parental permission, if given hesitantly, and my father, always good with his hands, had crafted me a green and gold mitre out of Bristol board and wrapping foil. I remembered my lines and delivered them with measured vigour. My forbearing mother even came to watch—a solitary figure among the other parents.

My mother and father had their limits, as things turned out. One Christmas Eve, inspired by I can't remember what—a movie, a book, simply years of pent-up envy and frustration—I decided to hang two pairs of stockings from the wobbly chest of drawers in my bedroom. It was a half-serious but hopeful gesture, a modest fantasy; but I must have had some strong reason to identify with the goyim that year because I do recollect a mounting, unprecedented sense of expectation. Christmas morning I was startled to find all the stockings filled. Oh, there was nothing fancy or worth more than a few dollars—half a dozen of my favourite comic books, some dime candy bars, two boxes of Oreos—but I was thrilled.

Indulged as I obviously knew myself to be—my father seemed most amused by the whole thing—I decided then and there that I would repeat the experiment the following year. When the time came I even added a third pair of socks. Christmas morning I awoke to find limp wool tacked to my weathered dresser, looking ridiculous and unmistakably accusing in a way I can't, to this day, find the right words to describe. It must have been a sight, my own face included, mirroring a concomitant feeling I wish on no child who has any legitimate business with Christmas. The stockings came down quickly and quietly, were folded and put away. Neither the house nor anyone in it ever breathed a word.

It was the end of borrowed magic. I had been reminded, not of what I was, but of what I was not. It was years before I dared to hang a stocking again.

The Christmas Dorothy Died

Wanda Robson

I often think of my parents and the balance they had to endure and navigate, with a very young family and grown children in the same house. In a family as big as ours—fifteen children, eleven that survived—the constant word was "share," and the ongoing struggle my parents had to face was the struggle to maintain balance among all the needs and differences. Almost like a scale for weighing jewels—the kind with two trays on a chain that dip to equal one another—I see the two rooms separated by sliding doors in my parents' house. The living room in front held a bare, undecorated Christmas tree and little children playing, waiting for Santa; and in the parlour on the other side of those doors my parents were preparing the body of their daughter Dorothy, who had just died.

All this had to be told to me. I was the youngest child, just eight days old when Dorothy died, Christmas Eve. This happened in 1926. Even though only a story, it seems like my memory, and I imagine my parents at that time, not young and not old—in the middle of so many lives, surrounded by family. Each older sister told some of the story to me later when I was in school. It's a sad story, but years later it was also a story my sister Viola Desmond was able to laugh about, as my sisters reminisced. Viola said, "Remember when we came down the street with all the parcels at Christmas!" Then I wanted to know what they were talking about.

And it turns out that it was December 24, 1926. I was eight

days old. And I was in a little crib by the bed where my sister Dorothy was. Dorothy was five years old. She wasn't convalescing, she was dying. And my mother knew that, my father knew that. They were told by the doctor six months before, that she had a disease they called peritonitis. I would say it was cancer, perhaps in the stomach lining. The doctor told my mother there was nothing more that they could do for her. My mother would have to get her out in the sun, bare her stomach to the sun. Perhaps that would help. But that was in the late spring or early summer when they told her that. And now it was winter.

I am told Dorothy said when I was born, "Oh, Mama, that will be my baby. Can I take care of her?" And Mum said, "You most certainly can."

My crib was right beside Dorothy's bed. And her bed activities were stringing beads and dressing her doll. My mother kept her doll and the beads.

This was the 24th of December in the house on 18 Swaine Street in Halifax where I was born.

My mother told me: "I was downstairs, stirring soup, getting supper ready." And she said, "I felt I had to go. I felt that there was something wrong." My mother told me this. And one of the girls was in the kitchen. "Where are you going, Mum?" She answered, "It's Dorothy. It's Dorothy." And Mum went into the room, Dorothy's room. I was in there in the crib. And she said Dorothy was sitting up, propped up with the pillows. She had the beads in her hand, where she was stringing them, and the doll by her side. She was dead.

My mother was upset, of course. She had been told of the imminent death. But I don't think a parent is ever fully prepared. You know it, perhaps. Perhaps you don't. But she really was extremely upset. She said, "Call your father, call your father. Somebody go get your father." And Dad came home.

They took Dorothy to the parlour, the rear side of the living room. They were double rooms. A living room here, the front room. I think years ago they called it a front and back parlour. And if something was going on, they had the sliding doors between them. So Dorothy was put in the back parlour.

Our minister came and prayed with Mum. And there was an organ in the corner. And I think—I'm not quite certain about this—I think Mum said she played one of Dorothy's little favourites, like "Jesus Loves Me"—a little child's hymn that they would like.

The doctor came in and pronounced her dead. They were getting Dorothy ready for her burial. And the little girls were running around in the living room, excited about Christmas, on the other side of the doors. And children were running upstairs.

My father and my mother told the older girls to go up and quiet the children upstairs, and try to explain to everyone, considering their ages, what had happened. So the older ones went upstairs. Years later I asked a sister, "Weren't you sad?" She said, "Of course, we all were sad. But my mother was very religious. And she prepared us, every step upon the way about how we might feel." She knew that when you're young, your feelings are just here one minute and gone the next. So she didn't expect little ones to sit down and weep and sob.

Because, it was Christmas Eve! And Santa Claus was coming! A week before that somebody had come to the door selling trees. And my older sister Helen said, "Oh, we have to have a tree." Mum said, "Oh, I don't know." Dorothy wasn't dead at the time, though she was languishing. These are old expressions that come to me: languishing. Sounds very Victorian, I think.

So they did have an uncooked turkey in the icebox and a bare tree in the living room—nothing on it. My mother had said, "I don't feel as if I want to bring out ornaments or things like that right now." That was before Dorothy died. She just didn't feel like it. She didn't have the spirit of Christmas.

My oldest sister Helen was possibly seventeen. My mother

asked her to get the little ones ready for bed. And Mum and Dad and the minister were in with Dorothy.

But my older sisters said to one another, "You know, this is not right. These kids are excited. What are we going to do?" And Helen said, "Look. I'll get the children ready for bed. We'll let them hang up their stockings." We had the stockings and Christmas decorations in boxes in the attic. They dug them out. They even had names on them.

So Helen said, "You leave it to me about putting the stockings up." But another sister said, "I don't know. Mum will think it's sacrilegious. It's not right to do this in the midst of death." So Viola went to Dad. She said something like, "Dad, this is a very sad day. But the little ones—they were waiting for Santa Claus. What can we do?" Dad said, "You leave it to me. I'll talk to your mother."

So he talked to Mum. No one knows what he said. But he must have said the right thing. Because she relented, and said that they could have Christmas, but they were to keep it low-key, and just remind the children that it is a festive season, but their sister had just died. That's a difficult thing to do. I would think almost impossible. You know, Santa Claus!

Helen said, "Okay. You two girls go, hurry. There's a turkey in the ice chest. I've got to start it." Helen cooked—she was the greatest cook. I think it was in her fingertips. And she prepared the turkey, while the other two went shopping for gifts.

They went to the stores, and as Viola said to me years later, "What a great thing! Everything was fifty percent off! The night before Christmas! We got so much stuff. We purchased gifts for everyone. Dad gave us what little money he had." They said, "Oh, we got even more than what we had hoped."

After my sisters left the stores: "We were bundled! We were coming down Chebucto Road towards Swaine Street, laden down with parcels, and laughing." And they looked around in the street. And our house was the only one dark, with the funeral crepe on the door. They told me that they noticed the gloominess and the darkness in the wreath on our door. One of them said, "It struck me, the contrast. I was so happy. Then all of a sudden it came over me just what had happened, and why there was such a difference to the other houses."

All the other houses were lit up with wreaths on the doors and lights or candles in the windows.

When they got in the house, there was a smell of cooking. And there was a little low hum of the organ in the parlour, where the door was closed. It was getting late. And it was the old-fashioned coal stove, a large bird roasting in the oven. You could feel the heat as soon as you got in the house. And it was so cold outside.

"We assigned each other tasks." Helen was to finish decorating the tree, in between getting the turkey ready. Viola was to wrap the presents, and another sister was to fill the stockings. "We worked really, really fast." Boxes that Mum had stored away marked "Christmas" were all carried down into the living room. "We knew that the children would be up earlier, because it was Christmas."

It just worked out so well. In the midst of all their sorrow—all this activity, this happy, festive occasion on one side of the sliding doors. And on the other side, there was organ music, and a child being prepared for burial. The minister coming and going. The soft organ music would stop occasionally as my mother knelt in prayer.

My father would come from the parlour every so often, and check to see what was going on in the living room.

I was eight days old. And we didn't leave that street until I was about seven years old. My brother and I would go outside and we'd look up at the moon. Sometimes there was a shadow, sometimes it was a full moon. Sometimes to my eyes the little shadow was like somebody sitting there.

I'd say, "Oh, look, Jackie! Dorothy's looking!"

And Mum said Dorothy was watching over us. My mother was very spiritual. Even to this day I can see her. And I can still picture us then: "Jackie, look! Look! There's Dorothy!" He'd say, "Yeah. I think that's Dorothy." We'd come in and tell Mum we saw Dorothy. In the moon. And we'd always say, "Hi, Dorothy! Hi, Dorothy! Mum, I saw Dorothy!"

Oidhche Na Calluinn

There are a good many men today (*this was written in 1972*) on Cape Breton who remember going out on a frosty winter evening to celebrate Oidhche Na Calluinn. They would set out in a small group or if there was a lot of territory to cover perhaps there would be two groups, one at each end of the district—and each group would have a leader who would take them door to door. Sometimes they would go on sleighs and bells would be ringing, and on stormy nights they would be on snowshoes. The occupants of each house they visited would see their lanterns and hear them but they would not open the door. For they would hear strange sounds and see from the window a strange, strange sight.

The leader of the band would be wrapped in a dried sheepskin pulled up around his head. He would be running with another man running behind him, beating on the skin and sending up a horrible rattling sound as they circled the house three times in the direction of the sun. Then they would come to the door and the leader would yell out the "Duan na Calluinn." When he came to the last lines the door would be opened and the people would give something—perhaps potatoes or mutton or beef, and it would go in a bag brought along to handle the goods.

Finally, they would all go to one house. It was usually a

home where the people were less fortunate than their neighbours. Perhaps the father had died or was ill and it did not look as though there would be much of a holiday season in that house. They would get pots boiling and take food from the bag and cook up a terrific feast. And there would be singing and perhaps a story, and the tables would be pushed aside and a fiddler would set the whole room to dancing. And a wonderful time would be had in this house where only hours before it did not look like such a fine time could possibly be had. And it would be the wee hours and a sharp frost for the merrimakers to take off again for home, leaving behind what was left of the food—often a supply for a long, long time.

As far as we have been able to discover, these wonderful rites were last carried out on Cape Breton about forty years ago in the 1920s—and they had retained many aspects of the ancient pagan ritual carried out among the Celts before recorded time. In the Highlands of Scotland it was a bullskin, not a sheepskin, the horns and the hooves still attached. The man wearing the skin ran around the house sunwise—*deiseil*—because the ancient Celts oriented all things according to the direction of the path of the sun, and to have gone contrary to this would have been considered unlucky. According to Carmichael's *Carmina Gadelica*, the line "descending at the door" refers to the time when the old Highland houses were built of local stone, with very thick walls. The thatch was attached not quite to the very outside of the wall, leaving a ledge for men to stand on when thatching. The bullman would presumably run sunwise around this ledge, because projecting from the wall would be a series of stones from the ground to the ledge, usually near the door. Carmichael adds that there were two skins, the one worn, the other carried in the pocket, a very small piece—and thus line seven of the poem: "*Craicionn Calluinn 'na mo phòcaid.*"

John Gregorson Campbell in his book *Witchcraft and Second Sight in the Highlands and Islands of Scotland* (1902) describes the disorderliness of the Calluin ritual and adds another aspect we have so far been unable to explain—another poem, presumably recited prior to the "Duan Na Calluinn." It went: "The New Year of the yellow bag of hide,/ Strike the skin (upon the wall),/ An old wife in the graveyard,/ An old wife in the corner;/ Another old wife beside the fire,/ A pointed stick in her two eyes,/ A pointed stick in her stomach,/ Let me in, open this."

This is quite far from the Calluinn as practised on Cape Breton—but much of its old form did survive here long after it had deteriorated in the Hebrides. Today in Scotland, on the 11th of January—Hogmanay, the old date of New Year—what is left of the Calluinn is a children's festival. They go door to door and recite a poem and receive a treat. On Cape Breton the ritual survived more in its old form because of changes that gave it a new lease on life. Specifically, it was infused with the spirit of giving traditionally associated with Christmas. In fact, while the people of the North River district continued to go out on the last night of the year, the people of the North Shore practised Oidhche Na Calluin on Christmas Eve.

The Calluinn Rhyme / Duan Na Calluinn as we got it from Scalpay (Harris) years ago:

I came here first of all,
To renew for you the Calluinn;
I need not tell you that
It was there from the time
   of my grandfather.
I'll go sunwise round the house
And I'll descend at the door.
The Calluinn skin in my pocket,
And good will be the smoke
   coming from it;
There's no one who will hold it
   to his nose
But won't be healthy all his life.
The man of the house will
   get it in his hands

Thàinig mis' an seo air tùs
A dh'ùrachadh dhuibh na Calluinn;
Cha ruiginn a leas siud innseadh,
Bha i ann bho linn mo sheanar.
Théid mi deiseil air an fhàrdaich
'S teàrnaidh mi aig an dorus.
Craicionn Calluinn 'na mo phòcaid,
'S maith an ceò a thig bho'n fhear ud;
Chan eil duine chuireas r'a shròin e
Nach bi e ri bheò dheth fallain.
Gheibh fear an tighe 'na làimh e
Gus a cheann a chur 's an teallach.
Théid e deiseil air na pàisdean,
Ach gu h-àraid gheibh a' bhean e.
Gheibh a' bhean e, 's i as fhiach e ...

To put its head in the fireplace.
He'll go sunwise round the children,
But over and above, the woman
    of the house will get it,
The woman of the house will get it,
    and she well deserves it . . .
The hand that dispenses the Calluinn.
Because of the drought
    in the countryside
We don't expect a drink.
One small thing that I refuse—
The tiny scabby potatoes.
We'll not take the bread
    without the butter.
And we'll not take the butter
    without the bread.
We'll take the cheese on its own
And how then could we be

Làmh riarachaidh na Calluinn.
Leis an tart a th'air an dùthaich
Chan eil dùil againn ri drama.
Aon rud beag a tha mi diùltadh,
Rùileagan a' bhuntàta charraich.
Cha ghabh sinn an t-aran gun an t-im
'S cha ghabh sinn an t-ìm gun an t-aran.
Gabhaidh sinn an càise leis féin
'S cia air éisd a bhitheamaid falamh
'S ma tha e againn r'a fhaotainn
Ma dh'fhaodas na cùm maill' oirnn.
'S fosgail an dorus 's leig a stigh sinn.

◆

    empty-handed
And if it's there for us to get it
If you may, do not detain us.
Open the door and let us in.

Christmas Island Christmas

Andrea Sachs

Step inside the Christmas Island post office in Nova Scotia and you will feel it immediately, a rush of holiday spirit that hits you like a swig of eggnog or a whiff of roasting chestnuts. Santa figurines in various poses adorn the shelves, and bowls of candy canes and jelly beans provide envelope lickers with a sweet reprieve. Seasonal cards hang from a string along the ceiling, prayer flags of a different denomination. And in the back left corner, a woman younger than Mrs. Claus and taller than an elf stamped the Christmas Island postmark on a tumbling stack of cards.

"The people who come here are so full of spirit," said postmistress Hughena MacKinnon, who during the season dons an apron inspired by a Santa suit. "They like to add the special touch of the Christmas Island post stamp."

If Christmas Island truly honored its namesake, the post office's special edition postmark would feature the image of the local Mi'kmaq man whose festive surname now appears on maps of Cape Breton Island, the northernmost part of Nova Scotia. Yet no purists made a ruckus when former postmistress Margaret Rose MacNeil proposed a pictorial postmark that played up the holly-jolly appellation. The first one came out in 1994, featuring a wreath encircled by the letters of the town. A Christmas Island tradition was born.

"We have different versions each year. We make design changes—we may take away the leaves or add ornaments. We've had a Christmas tree coming out of an envelope and holly on a mailbox," said MacKinnon, a Cape Breton native who replaced MacNeil 12 years ago. "But we like to stay with the wreath. I like its message of wishing for good health."

The post office stands alone, a solitary box set back from a rural road, with unfettered views of Christmas Island pond and a small island overrun by nature. Occasionally, a car drives by. Frequently, that car stops outside the front door. In the absence of a diner, a bar or a barbershop, the post office has become a giant water cooler, where locals swap news and good wishes.

The Christmas Island post office serves 140 families, but once the stamp is released in mid-November, business explodes. (They keep it around until mid-January.) MacKinnon said she receives up to ten times as much mail during the holidays. In a record holiday season (1996-97), she processed 23,000 cards. Once, the lieutenant governor dropped off 2,500 envelopes over two days. This season, she expects to hand-stamp 14,000 to 17,000 pieces.

On the 23rd day before Christmas, the morning count was in the low triple digits—a slow day, according to MacKinnon. To maintain some order, she kept the pile of envelopes addressed to the post office in a box, which contained numerous cards that needed the finishing touch. On top of that, visitors stopped by throughout the day to drop off their loads, often carried in multiple plastic bags.

"Let me shake your hand. I have always wanted to meet you," exclaimed Cathy Finney, who had driven an hour south, her husband in tow. "Every year, we say we are going to do this. This year, we were determined to do it."

Finney left behind twenty-four cards and a warm handprint on MacKinnon's palm.

While MacKinnon tended to customers at the counter, I nominated myself her elf and dug into the paper mounds. I ripped open envelopes, shaking the packages before placing the cards over by the workstation with ink pads and two stamps (one red, one green). Often the senders include a personal note to Mac-Kinnon, expressing their gratitude on decorative stationery or the lip of the envelope.

"We really appreciate the wonderful work you do and the joy it brings to the recipients of the cards when they see that they have been sent from Christmas Island," read one note. In another, she received a gift of Year of the Tiger stamps, with the inscription: "A few stamps for your kindness."

"Maybe he thought I would run out," she quipped.

Following MacKinnon's instructions, I pressed one wreath on the actual stamp and another on a clean part of the envelope, in case collectors wanted a pure form for their books. Advance apologies to those whose wreaths turned out half-formed, too light, lopsided or too smudgy.

Before the post office closed for lunch, I pulled out one of my own Christmas cards and slid it over to MacKinnon for a one-two stamp. I was going to spread Nova Scotia's holiday spirit by first-class mail.

Reporter Laura Jean Grant writes on the *Cape Breton Post* website,

"The holiday crunch is on at Canada Post locations across the country, and perhaps no post office feels it more keenly than in the rural Cape Breton community of Christmas Island. There, thousands of letters and packages are sent each Christmas season by people looking to have their holiday mail stamped with the distinctive and festive Christmas Island postmark."

Christmas Island postmistress Hughena MacKinnon is quoted in the piece as saying, "They come from all over Canada, we get them from the States, we get them from several countries around the world. A lot of stamp collectors and that, like to get the postmark for Christmas. We usually do in the vicinity of 10,000 Christmas cards per season hand-stamped with our postmark, and that's just the cards alone, not packages and parcels and everything else. Usually, our busiest day, we do about 1,000 per day, when Christmas gets close in December."

From a talk with Hughena MacKinnon, Postmistress, Christmas Island

The late Margaret Rose MacKenzie MacNeil was the one who was responsible for starting the pictorial postmark. When Margaret Rose was postmistress, there were always people who came up from Sydney to have their Christmas cards stamped with the Christmas Island postmark. And Margaret Rose asked Canada Post if there was something she could do to make it a little special for these people. And that's where we became one of the first ones in Canada—I don't know if we were the first but pretty close—to have a pictorial postmark.

Rod Farrell, the Christmas Island Mail Driver, added: She'd dress up in period costume of the old days, during Christmas season.

Hughena: She received the Order of Canada for public service.

And now, we not only have people who come every year—we have people who came for decades. We have people who make their own cards, draw their own cards—and we put the postmark on it, the final touch—and off it goes.

We use the regular postmark with three Christmas Trees on the island that we use during the regular months, till about mid-November. Then we start using the pictorial ones. But we put them on postcards in the summertime if a collector requests them.

A couple of years ago they did an article in the Toronto paper in the Chinese script, then it was in the paper in British Columbia, and after that we got quite a few requests from Hong Kong and China and Korea, looking for the postmark. People will put two cards in an envelope or if they have twenty cards they put it in a box—and they will have them all addressed with the proper postage put on them, each one. And once we get their cards, we postmark the stamps and send them off the same day.

We've been running over a thousand envelopes a day, with Evelyn MacKinnon helping—and that's hand stamped. And usually what we will have to do—we will have to cancel the stamp and you'd have a half image or something like that. Then we'd usually stamp a clear image as well. So usually people will have the red and green one. And the reason we have red and green is that a lot of the Christmas cards have red or green envelopes, so you have to have the other colour to show up.

These postmarks are official. The government makes them up—Canada Post. They've gone back to the original design by stamp designer Stephen Slipp.

(*So if I had 500 friends, or even a hundred—addressed them, sealed the envelopes, put a hundred envelopes into a box, and I mailed them to Christmas Island post office—you would open the box and hand stamp the postage stamps and mail them. You say, perhaps a thousand a day.*)

We usually do—the last couple of years—say 14,000 to 16,000 cards per holiday season—just the cards. That's not counting the parcels and the other things.

We did 2200 cards in one day. We knew they were coming. They were all the Lieutenant Governor of Nova Scotia's Christmas cards going out—1,600 were his. We mailed Senator Buchanan's. Gordie Gosse usually comes up every year. And that's usually 500 cards in one day.

And when the elementary school was here—the little ones would come down with their Santa letters—and we'd have candy for them and they each had an envelope where they got to put the postmark, a red mark and a green mark, and take that home as a souvenir.

Once stamped, the envelopes are taken separately from the rest of the mail stream and forwarded through the Halifax plant without getting any additional stamping which might spoil the image.

You can't say this is a thankless job because just about everyone has a note thanking you for the work you do.

To get the Christmas Island postmark on your mail, send your addressed cards with proper postage in a larger envelope to Christmas Island Post Office, Grand Narrows Highway, Christmas Island, N.S. B1T 1A0.

Christmas Eve at the Sydney Steel Plant

Paul MacDougall

Nobody was drinking too much but we were drinking. After all it was Christmas Eve and the brick suppliers had just been by and left a case of forties in the general office building. The super was a sour old lot but he scoffed two bottles for us and away we went. First stop was the rail mill. Those guys had shut down last week for repairs. They did that every Christmas so we knew there'd be some laughs to be had over there. Sure enough Johnny Mac was there with his tinsel.

Johnny'd been injured or some such thing years ago, no one can even remember or even cared anymore, but he'd got himself a honeyman job. You know, something easy, not too laborious, that kind of work. He'd spent the better part of the year saving cigarette paper foils and twisting them into tinsel. It was everywhere now. Every Sid, Ray and Johnny on the plant with a tree in his shack had some of Johnny's homemade Export A tinsel dangling from it by now, that and coils of copper wire made into ornaments by the guys in the electrical shop. A drink or two and a laugh or two and we were off once again.

The snow was just starting to fall and put everyone in the mood when someone shouted across the yard that the copper recyclers were just over at number one gate. We were off like a flash. These guys were always creeping round the plant taking bits and pieces of copper pipe and wire and any old copper doodad they could scrounge up that may be worth a few cents. Those few cents added up to thousands by the end of the year, so today was payback day. Drinks for everyone. It was just getting dark enough and with the snow and all, a luster appeared on the big Christmas tree on top of the gate.

All the trees were lit up by then. The big one on the general office building appeared to my eyes like a vision from on high. The electricians had done another fine job of setting the lights on that one as well as the huge wooden one on top of the blast furnace. How she never caught fire we'll never know. It had to be the only Christmas tree with the Star of David on it. Something for all seasons, and for all people, we guessed.

"We just saw Santa head into the general office building," someone said. "Well we're not going there," I replied. "He's probably going to give a boss a raise. We're off to the white house." The electricians had a luxury shack at the plant complete with a full kitchen set up and a guy in there who would rather cook than work. You cook my goose and I'll protect yours, was the rule. Those guys did it all up fancy, complete with turkey, turnips, potatoes, the whole Christmas meal. No need to miss this.

There was a pile of fellas in there when we pranced in. It's funny but this time of the year was the only time when you got to talk to some of the other folks who worked on the plant. Other times you just went to your work and did it. But for a day or two at Christmas the company turned a blind eye and let everyone enjoy themselves. As long as the furnaces didn't go completely out, everybody was happy. Everyone was wishing everyone else Merry Christmas in their native tongues. Buono Natale, Nollaig Chridheil, Wesolych Swait, Veseloho Vam Rizda, and on and on it went.

Everyone was talking and chattering to everyone.

"How she's goin' b'y?"

"Good, how you doin'?"

"Where ya goin' tonight?"

"Heading to Midnight Mass at St Nicholas."

"Cooking your turkey at home or having the baker do it?"

"The Missus brought it to Bernie's this morning. Lot easier to have him do it in the big brick pizza oven than let me do it in the coke ovens, like last year."

We were full when we left, like a couple of jolly old elfs, and decided to call it a day. The guys who didn't drink were all hanging around the gate waiting to take those of us home who did. It was all good fun and someone was always looking out for you, like you would for them. After all it was Christmas Eve at the steel plant, we truly were a family, and everything was all right.

A Latvian Immigrant's Note of Thanks

Andris Kundzins

December 24, 1949

I am not a story writer but at this time I have to make an exception and tell everyone my true story about our first Christmas in this country. This is the best way to thank, once more, all those people who made that Christmas a special and unforgettable one for us.

I came to Canada forty years ago to work for J.W. Stephens, a building supply and construction company in Sydney. It was one of the two largest building companies in Cape Breton, located on Townsend Street, where the railroad tracks cut through the city.

Nine months after my arrival, my family—my wife and fifteen-month-old daughter, and mother-in-law—were coming to join me. Their boat was due to arrive in Halifax just before Christmas.

Before I left for Halifax to meet them, Greg, the company accountant, suggested that a set of my apartment keys be left with him so that in case of a cold spell he could look after the water pipes.

The boat with my family arrived on Christmas Eve and we spent the night on the train travelling to Sydney. On the morning of Christmas Day, tired but happy, we arrived at our apartment.

As we entered it, we could not believe our eyes. On the table there was a nice little Christmas tree decorated with lights and all the trimmings. Next to it was a box with a turkey and everything else needed for a full Christmas dinner. All this was from the office staff. We were overwhelmed!

Now, after forty years remembering our many previous Christmases, our first Christmas in this country seems to be the most remembered, thanks to you—Greg, Ed, Jeff, Agnes, Delores, Barett, Sandy and the others. Merry Christmas to all of you and your families.

Hong Kong Fell on Christmas Day, 1941

Austin Roberts

You know people who tell you they were patriotic, and they joined up because they wanted to save the country—you know, that's mostly BS, to tell you the truth. Most people joined up because they were so damned poor. At that time—1939—I know that, watching them come into the recruiting station, there were more came in with a pair of overalls with the seat worn out of them, and maybe a pair of sneakers on, or an old pair of something on their feet. That's everything they owned, you know. And that's why they joined up. I guess maybe there might have been a bit of feeling into it, too, but most of it was practical.

I served in the Far East—Hong Kong. We left Vancouver. It took us twenty-three days to get down there—November 13. (*Did you know where you were headed?*) No idea. The only thing they told us was—after we left the Philippines, a couple of days from China—they told us that war could break out any minute, and it might be bad enough that we'd have a job to get off the ship. We weren't at war yet. War for us—the war in the Pacific—started on the 8th of December, 1941.

We knew that the war in Europe was going on strong. But the Japanese hadn't declared war yet. We were getting guns set up along the island of Hong Kong, on the shores. We had 2200 men. Our outfit had ten miles of coastline to cover. Well, 2200 men, you spread them along ten miles, and you don't get too many in one spot.

The morning of the 8th of December—I came out of breakfast, and I had two mess tins. I had washed them and I was shaking them, drying them out.

First thing, you could hear the roar of the planes coming. And you knew there were a lot of them. I just looked out for a minute and, boy, they were coming hell for leather, all these bombers. And the Japanese bombed the damn place flat. They got every plane that was on the airport, and every building that was around anywhere—they bombed her flat.

The British are great troops, best in the world. I don't care what anybody says, there's nothing can touch a British troop. They fought there, but they were overrun with men and guns and tanks and stuff—they didn't have a hope in hell. The Japanese kept driving them back and driving them back and driving them back. Once they got down to Kowloon, then they could make a crack at the island of Hong Kong.

The first night, they just sort of took a little stab at it, to see what would happen. But our old colonel was pretty cute. He got a whole bunch of 45-gallon barrels of oil—high octane is what it was—gasoline. Hauled them out into the harbour a ways with little boats, and buoyed them there. I remember that day; we worked like slaves. It was a hell of a hard place to work in. The temperature down there is not like here—it seems to press down on you.

Anyway, we put these barrels out. I suppose we put about 200 of them out altogether. And that night the Japanese made a real attempt to come across. Once they got in amongst the barrels, we turned the mortars on the barrels. We had quite a fire for a while. Boats and men and water and the whole damn works, you know, went up in flames. There was no way they could get out of it. So that attempt failed.

From that morning of the 8th of December till December 25th, we never had a sleep. As I said, we had 2200 men to start with, and that beach to cover. An attack on any part of it, you had to rush there. It wasn't just a flat beach—this was mountains and hills and swamp, and everything that made it hard to move in. See, you were on the move continuously, all the time, back and forth, back and forth—trying to defend this place and that place.

That's where we spent eighteen days of actual combat. Never managed a rest of any kind, shape, or form. Eighteen days—we never got to sit down and have a rest. You'd go to sleep standing up, fall down sometimes. And they just kept pushing us and banging us and hammering us.

I had put on a new pair of boots the morning before the war started. And you know, when the battle ended on Christmas Day, after eighteen days of fighting, I had a hole in both soles of those boots. That's how much we travelled. They'd try to attack one spot. We'd all rush there to beat them back. And in the meantime they'd be trying in another spot. And you'd have to rush from that spot over to the next spot to try again.

We were in a compound in Stanley Village Christmas Day. We went in there the night before. Compound would be, I'd say, three acres at the outside. On Christmas Day, they dropped and fired a thousand and ten bombs and shells on that area on that day. Now we were dug down into the basements and everywhere we could get dug in. Every fellow just hunted a hole and crawled into it. Myself, I went into a sewerage thing, under the road. Other fellows did the same, under everything.

On one side of the island of Hong Kong, there was this city of Hong Kong itself. Two million people into it. They didn't attack Hong Kong City at all. They were attacking all around, clear of that. They had good logic for not doing it. You'll find out.

Anyway, as I say, they got a foothold in Stanley Village. That's how come we were in these different houses, trying to dislodge them and get rid of them. So it went on, back and forth and back and forth and back and forth and back and forth. Every now and then a plane would go over and drop leaflets saying, "Give up. Give up, and we'll all be friends," sort of. And of course, we didn't want to be friends. We wanted to see what we could do. Anyway, this contingent of Canadians—2200—in one sense we were there under British rule. We had our own brigadier and everything, but still the British were actually the head bosses.

So on December the 21st they gave the British commander an ultimatum: "Quit. Or we'll bomb the city of Hong Kong." Now, you have two million people you're responsible for, in a sense, eh? They gave them so long for an answer. Tried to haul it out as long as they could. But on December the 24th, the man that was in charge of the British forces in Hong Kong surrendered the island to the Japanese.

There was a lull for three or four hours—until they found out that the Canadians hadn't surrendered. They gave the same ultimatum to the Canadians; the Canadians said, "Go to hell. The only way we'll surrender is if you guarantee you'll take prisoners." 'Cause they didn't plan on taking any prisoners. And they said, No, they wouldn't do that. So it went on and on and on and on. On Christmas Day, now, December the 25th, we were in an area of ruined buildings, just bits and pieces of buildings here and there. And when dark came, we came out to fight again. They sent a bunch—they sent a feeler in to see what happened, and we blew them away again. So they sent in a white flag, then, to talk to the colonel. They took messages back and forth.

At twelve o'clock on Christmas Day, the Canadians surrendered. But they had a guarantee that at least we would be taken prisoners, not shot. That was December the 25th, 1941.

(*What did you do for Christmas that year?*) Went to sleep. Each and everybody. One of the buglers blew a bugle and announced that there had been a surrender. I remember—three of us had a hole dug, we were in. We just looked at one another and laid down and went to sleep, the three of us. Nothing to say, and just so tired that you didn't care what the hell had happened. You had done all you could do, and that was it.

Sandy's Cape Breton Pork Pies

Cape Breton pork pies are date-filled tarts topped with a citrus butter icing. Sandy introduced me to them when I was but a lad. Since then, Christmas/Festivus hasn't been Christmas/ Festivus without a Cape Breton pork pie. This recipe is quick, and enjoyably messy.

The recipe should make roughly 30 mini tarts.

Shells
1 cup butter
4 tablespoons icing sugar
2 cups flour (I use 1 cup bleached all-purpose flour and 1 cup whole wheat all-purpose flour)
Prepare yourself a glass of Bailey's and milk.
Mix the flour and icing sugar.
Cut the butter into small cubes and knead it into the flour. Within a few minutes, you'll get a greasy ball. Press the dough into small muffin tins. When you're pressing you can make the

shell quite thin (3 or 4 millimetres)—it will expand impressively as it cooks.

Bake at 425° F. for 10 minutes. Cool before filling.

Filling

>2 cups tightly packed chopped brown dates
>¾ cup brown sugar
>1 ½ cups water
>lemon juice of half a lemon

Enjoy a glass of rum and eggnog (if you have a little coffee and nutmeg, toss those into your drink for good measure).

Simmer the ingredients together until they get a soft, mushy consistency. Allow to cool. Fill shells.

Icing

The icing makes the pie. It should be citrus-y and sweet. Sandy's recipe didn't include her mix for the icing, so I've had to reverse engineer it. With a little help from the intarwebs, this is my current knock-off:

>½ cup butter
>1 ½ cups icing sugar
>1 tablespoon milk
>juice of half a lemon (you can add more)
>1 ½ teaspoons vanilla extract

You'll need your wits for this bit, so mix a little rum or irish cream into hot chocolate and savour that before beginning.

Cube the butter and knead it into the icing sugar. Mix the milk, lemon juice, and vanilla together with a spoon and beat it like it owes you money. You'll end up with a thick sugary gooey mass. Add a little more icing sugar to give it some body. This recipe makes about twice as much icing as you'll need, so find some way to enjoy the remainder.

Top the tartlets with the icing.

Store the tartlets in the fridge. The icing can turn to goo and pour off if you aren't careful.

Nova Scotia's $1.38-a-Day Laborer and His Family

J.B. McLachlan

A scrap of paper comes down to us, barely surviving. The microfilm captures what is left of the page. It is 1906. It is labor leader J.B. McLachlan writing to the editor of *The Halifax Herald*, reprinted in *The Labor Herald* newspaper. A few words are missing. The meaning is clear.

To the Editor
of *The Halifax Herald*

Sir,—As we approach December 25th, our minds turn to Him who is the greatest of all men who have appeared on this earth. His greatness appeared in this: that He refused to rise above His people in material things, and taught emphatically that no man had a right to ask other men to shoulder a burden that they themselves would not move with one of their fingers, and that those who were greatest ought to be servants of all. To preach economics of that kind is to preach the very antithesis of what is practiced today. At this Christmas time, I want to put up a plea for a little more justice and mercy for the poor and heavy-ladened in this province who are known by the unkindly name of "cheap labor." Let us take a man that earns $1.38 per day. On such a wage a man with a wife and family of say, five children, must work every day he can. Let the number of days worked in the year be 300. That would give him $414 a year.

See how he lives, how he fares, on such a wage and ask which of his instructors, preacher or politician—who generally tell this poor man that it is his own thriftlessness and lack of industry that keeps him poor—would step into his overalls for one year in order to give him a practical lesson in thrift, industry, and economics. Or will either dare to say that they could teach this poor man anything about these virtues?

Three hundred days work at $1.38 per day gives $414. He spends on rent, each year, $30; coal and light, $16; insurance for seven persons, $19; taxes, $3; doctor, $4.60; postage and newspapers, $3.50; washing and laundry, $8; boots for man, $3.50; boots for woman, $1.50; boots for five children, $7.50; outside clothes for man, $8; outside clothes for woman, $8; outside clothes for five children, $13.90; underwear for man, $1.40; underwear for woman, $1.40; underwear for five children, $7; school books, $4; general household wear, $2; Total, $142.30; which leaves him a balance of $271.70 for food for one year. Or to each of this family of seven, $38.81. Or 10 ½ cents to provide for each of these seven, for each day of the year. Or three meals a day at 3 ½ cents a piece.

This man spends nothing on rum, church, theatre, politics, or trades unionism. A daily paper for himself, a few toys for his children, or fifty cents spent on a little present for his wife, are luxuries beyond his reach. He leads a dull, joyless, laughterless life, that is one tragic struggle against want. He generally occupies a house of the shack or hovel description set upon the worst piece of land in his neighborhood. Not only is he robbed of the wealth that he creates, but is insulted by having free lectures thrust upon him about thrift and industry by trade union leaders and clergymen, who generally don't get out of bed in the morning for hours after this poor man is in the harness.

It is said that "God giveth to all men liberally, and upbraideth not." This province, on account of the "great need for cheap labor," cannot afford to treat the dollar-thirty-eight man liberally, nor can the preacher or the politician afford to let the poor man believe that his poverty is caused by anything else than his lack of industry and thrift. We trade unionists at least might refrain from asking this man to come into our union in order to get lessons on thrift and industry. We might leave to the men who never take off their coats the job of insulting this poor man, by asking him to do the impossible.

To me it appears that Carlyle put such as this dollar-thirty-eight man in his right place, when he said, "Two men I honor, and no third. First, the toil-worn craftsman that with earth-made implement laboriously conquers the earth and makes her man's. Venerable to me is the hard hand, crooked, coarse, wherein, notwithstanding lies a cunning virtue, indefeasibly royal, as of the sceptre of this planet. Venerable, too, is the rugged face, all weather-tanned, besoiled, with its rude intelligence; for it is the face of a man living manlike. O, but the more venerable for thy rudeness, and even because we must pity as well as love thee! Hardly-entreated brother! For us was thy back so bent, for us were thy straight limbs and fingers so deformed; thou wert our conscript, on whom the lot fell, and fighting our battles wert so marred."

A MINER.
Sydney Mines

Merry Christmas to You, Jim

Dawn Fraser

Jim McLachlan spent Christmas of 1923 in prison—sentenced for sedition because he said, "When you put the property of the Dominion Coal Company on one scale and the wives and children of workers earning thirty cents an hour on the other, then I say—the property of Dominion Coal Company can go to hell!"

Cape Breton's Christmas

I spent Christmas night of that year in a flop-house in another part of the country. Because accommodations were so poor, and perhaps because I had no supper, I could not sleep, and while I was in this uncomfortable position the fairies attacked me: "Merry Christmas to you, Jim; Merry Christmas to you, Jim; In your prison dungeon dim; In your prison dungeon dim," came pouring into my head as clearly as if someone was speaking in the room. I realized from past experience that I had to do my stuff, but I was handicapped. There was no electric or gas light in the room and only an old-fashioned lamp was available. I found a match and pencil, but did not have a scrap of paper. "Write it on the wall, write it on the wall," commanded the fairies, pausing in their dictation. That's what I did—wrote the following lines on the smooth board unpainted wall of the flop-house. The lines are probably there still, if the flop-house is: "Merry Christmas to you, Jim, In your prison dungeon dim. . . ."

Merry Christmas to you, Jim,
In your prison dungeon dim;
What although the bars are cold,
They have sheltered hearts of gold,
Fit companions they for you—
Steel is strong and steel is true.
Ah, better, yes with you to stand
Than humbly lick a tyrant's hand,
Like slaves and traitors to the cause
Who pawn their souls
        for men's applause;
The steel were truer friend
        than him—
Merry Christmas to you, Jim.

The meanest, vilest dungeon hole
Can never stain an honest soul,
And prison stripes can't
        dim your star,
It's not where you are,
        but what you are.
Persecute you all they can,

But, Jim McLachlan, you're a man,
And by the God whom I adore,
I'd rather pace a prison floor
And sleep in dungeons dark and cold
Than sell my soul for Besco's gold;
His masters must be proud of him—
Merry Christmas to you, Jim.

The mines are as they
        have ever been,
Kids are starving 'round Sixteen—
Ah, but blessed are the meek,
Blessed with two shifts a week.
Paper buncombe is the same,
But now they don't know
        who to blame.
Before you went and broke the laws,
Jim McLachlan was the cause
Of all the sin, distress and crime
That might occur in modern time,
But now they can't blame it on him—
Merry Christmas to you, Jim.

Christmas on Scatarie Island

Mame and Joe Spencer

We'd have great fun there in the wintertime. Skate, play hockey, play cards and shoot guns. Cut our own wood through the winter. *Mame*: September and during October we used to have raffles, dances—sell the raffles and kill the sheep and raffle that. (*Did you feel locked off from the rest of the world?*) No. If all the families were back there again, I'd just as soon be back to Scatarie as anywhere.

Joe: So would I. More fun back there. On the pond skating all day. Heavy breeze of wind. Had a sail on your back—was six feet across—go up and down the pond about a mile long. Gale of wind be on that sail and that sail on your back—you'd go some too, wouldn't you? When it would keep blowing you'd go before it, out the harbour road going sixty miles an hour. Boy, you'd drive her. And we had ice boats—make ice boats. Take a piece of plank across this way—with skates and a piece of iron behind for a rudder. Put a spar and sit on her. Be good, but you had to be careful.

Mame: And they used to have—I guess you never heard tell— the Mummers. Came when the Newfoundland people arrived there. Well I think they still have that yet in Newfoundland. Something like Halloween, only different.

Joe: During Christmastime you would dress up. Make a mask and dress up. Go from house to house. Good time.

Mame: Only then they'd have my dear lovely rigs down there. Go around and then at the last house probably they'd take off their faces, sit down and talk. When they had the mask on, you'd try to pick them out. If you did know you wouldn't exactly bring their names out—you know, you'd make them feel bad, they'd have to go somewhere else.

Joe: I did a lot of it. You'd draw your mask to suit yourself. *Mame*: Probably some put a suit of underwear on. Men probably dress like women. Women's clothes and shoes. I'll tell you the truth, boy, it was fun. One or two o'clock in the morning before they'd be gone on their way.

(*Is this little children?*) Oh no. *Joe*: Fifteen years old, sixteen. *Mame*: Oh my dear, some were in their thirties and forties.

Joe: We started about a week before Christmas. We wouldn't buy false faces at all. Get cotton and paint it up and make our own faces.

Clem Spencer: Some bad faces, too. Scary faces. Used to take a bird and skin it and turn the feathers inside and skin outside and cut holes and paint it—and with the feathers, it would be all like pimples all over the face.

Joe: Dress up as ugly as we could. Probably ten of us, dressed up—and another fellow with a fiddle. Mouth organ. Anything at all. Went to every house on the island. Dance. Wouldn't say very much because they'd know your voice. When you're a Mummer you try to talk different than you used to talk. We'd have a great time. They'd have to guess you.

Try to get your shape sometimes—you're twisting. Have to figure out who you'd be. Every Christmas.

Come a heavy snowstorm then we wouldn't go—but clear of that. Dancing and singing, lots of booze around. *Mame*: We just sung Christmas songs, and some would sing the odd hymn and some would sing little rhymes—not too much. Afraid if you sang too much they'd catch on—they knew them all so well.

They'd do the work in the daytime and at night this would take place. And not very often on Sunday. With bad weather, you'd get six or seven days out of it. *Joe*: Went dressed in an overcoat down to East Point one time—long walk for her. Had my shoes on I guess. She was dressed as a man and I had her clothes on and her shoes—so you know what kind of a shape my feet was into.

Mame: Today if you dressed up, come up here, they'd call the Mountie, think you're foolish.

A Christmastime Walk

Stephen W. MacNeil

I was trying to tell the hardships the first settlers suffered and did in this country, you know, how they stuck it out and lived here. In the wilderness with nothing much to live on.

There's a story regarding that, regarding this man, MacIntyre, that found the Glengarry mineral spring.

My grandfather, MacIsaacs, they lived down here, you can see them from the main road. That's where they landed and that's where they lived. Well, this man MacIntyre came from Scotland afterwards and all the land was taken up, but he went right back there, about seven miles inland from the main road, right out to the mineral spring. And it seems this fall that the potatoes failed for everybody, there was a blight or something struck and killed the crops—and there wasn't too much for them to eat more than hemp, I guess.

Well anyway, his wife was a weaver from Scotland. She weaved cloth. And she weaved what they call a bolt—forty yards, you know—and she weaved that, and he tied it on his back and he started in and he stopped at my great-grandfather's—on his way to North Sydney to sell this warp of cloth for to get something to eat.

And so he went to North Sydney. And it was late fall and the freeze-up was after coming in, and all this cloth that was weaved by the first settlers around here went to Newfoundland to make clothes for fishermen, you know. And when he got to North Sydney, the freeze-up came and there was no travel, no way of sending the stuff to Newfoundland. He couldn't sell it, couldn't get a nickel for it. Had to walk back to my grandfather's place [at Big Pond] down here—and not a bite to eat, only they kept him while he was there, I guess.

But he told my grandfather or told them all, I guess, to go out and tell his wife—take something with them, too, I guess, to feed them—that he was going to Arichat the next day. It was an open port then, Arichat—it wouldn't freeze up—and he thought that there'd be a possibility of selling the cloth in Arichat.

So my grandfather went out and told MacIntyre's wife the story.

Well anyway, MacIntyre walked to Arichat. When he got to Arichat, same story verbatim: he couldn't sell it, couldn't give it away. So he walked back and went to my grandfather's place down there. And my grandfather's brother was after in—and he was working in Halifax at something—and he came home during while all this was going on, you know. I guess he came home for Christmas, that he'd be home for Christmas, the young fellow. My grandfather then would be only about sixteen when he was travelling back and forth.

So my grandfather's brother pitied the old fellow, he pitied MacIntyre. And he had a little money and he bought the cloth, bought this roll from MacIntyre there, and MacIntyre was happy as a clam.

He told my grandfather to go out again and tell his wife that he was going to North Sydney again. 'Course he went with the money this time, and got fifty pounds of meal, flour, whatever made it up of fifty pounds of something to eat, anyway, tied it on his back and came back there to my grandfather's place with it and a bottle of gin.

And the next day he went home.

"I remember Lon and footsteps in the snow"

Kenneth Bagnell

In the village I come from, and have never really left, there is a house, weathered by the wind and in sight of the sea.

It has been there these many years, alone in a great field. Behind it are two sheds, a barn and then, stretching into the distance like a green, silent ocean, is the forest. In front is an empty field, its grass brown and hard and dusted with snow. And a mile away is the boiling winter sea.

It is a morning in the middle of December, over twenty years ago, and in the house are a man, a woman and a small boy. The man and woman are in their sixties and the boy is seven. He is not their child, for they have none.

But he is their friend—their special friend—and he comes to see them so often that they call him, not by his name, but simply Dear. It will always be that way, even after he is grown and gone away and does not come much anymore. I am that boy.

The woman, whose name is Maggie, is tall, with a remarkable face, strong and craggy, with deep dark flashing eyes and hair that is black and shiny and swept to the back of her head. The man is called Lon, and like the sound of his name, he is soft and gentle, with a face that is round and unwrinkled.

I am with them today, as I am every winter at this time, because school is closed for the Christmas recess. And I have come to the village to be with my grandparents and my ten aunts and uncles who live in a big house across the field from Maggie and Lon. Maggie is my grandmother's sister; Lon is my grandfather's brother.

Every morning, after breakfast, I pull on my britches and my cap with the leather ear lugs and run across the field, past the well that is sheathed with ice, along the footpath where the dead grass cracks beneath my feet, and rap on the porch door.

And the greeting is always the same, "Well, dear! It's time again." It is always that way, year after year. I wait all fall and then a day comes, a cold birdless day, and it is time for my friend and me to head off each morning for our special adventure.

We go to the woods behind the house, the great friendly forest, its spruce trees straining beneath burdens of snow and its floor soft with whiteness. We are, of course, looking for a tree, but that is secondary. My friend and I are setting snares for rabbits. We love these woods for we pick blueberries here every summer and we know all its paths. Some of them lead to bootleg pits that are old and falling in, where people climb down on ladders to dig coal to burn all winter. We pass them often in summer on the way to a beach where I can swim and he knows I am safe. Sometimes we take a lunch in a cracker box and I leave the box in the woods just to see how long it will last. Once I saw the same box in the same spot for three winters.

My friend and I travel well together in the woods, for I am small and cannot easily move when the snow is deep. And he is slow, too, for he is bent over from being badly hurt, not once, but twice in his life. When only ten years old he went to work in the coal mine. There, when he was in his twenties, his back was broken. Years later, a huge stone fell on him, crushing him and trapping him alone for many hours. He barely lived and never worked again.

We never talk of that. Mostly it is of Christmas and how it was when he was small and buying his first Christmas gifts for his father and mother. He made, he said, only forty cents a day and so for Christmas, he had to save for many weeks to buy the gifts he wanted.

He asks always about my school work and I think it strange that he never uses the word "grade," but "book." "What book are you in now, dear?" he will ask. Or else, "You should go on to the last book, dear, and then perhaps you'll go to college."

When we get to the deepest part of the forest, he tells me to keep behind him and to walk in his steps. I put my feet in the places he makes in the snow and we go to our favourite clearing and set out snares. He carefully pulls down the branches and I hand him the twine and he slowly ties the snare.

Then each morning we go back, and always, year after year, I follow him, as he tells me to, in his tracks in the snow. I think of the story of King Wenceslas and his page and we laugh and pretend that like the king whose steps were warm for his page, my friend warms the cold winter snow for me.

One morning I awake with a sore throat and cannot get up. But I hear him in the kitchen below at the first glimmer of dawn. My throat is so sore I cannot speak and so I watch from my window as he crosses the field, crawls beneath the fence and disappears in the forest. Before noon he is back and slowly climbs to my room and sits on the bed to show me the rabbit in my snare.

No day passes in all those years that we do not find at least one rabbit. I will not know until I grow up that each night he returns alone to the snares with a rabbit he bought at the store and if none have been caught, he puts one there so I shall not be disappointed.

When Christmas comes, I open my gifts at my grandparents' and then once again I cross the field in the winter stillness to see my friend. He sits at the window, looking and waiting, and waves to me and when I enter he sweeps me into his arms and I tell him of the wonders of the morning. He listens like a child, for in a way, he has remained a child.

One year I get a pair of skates and he comes with me while I try them out on a patch of ice in the field. He stays there, leaning with both hands on an old cane with a knob on top, until the sun goes down and the lights go on and the moon silvers the woods. "You are doing wonderful, dear," he says. And we cross the snow to the house and Aunt Maggie gives us peppermints and we all sit there in the quiet of Christmas night until finally he begins to nod.

Life comes between us. I go away to college to become, as he hoped I would, a minister, and he and Maggie give me all they can: a roll of old church papers they think might help me prepare sermons. Now and then I come back and take services in the little church in the village and they are there, no matter how hard it is to climb the steps, and he says to me afterward as he said years before, "You are doing wonderful, dear."

All his life he is teaching me the lesson I shall know, but not always heed: That ultimately it is better to be good than clever.

Finally comes a day when he can no longer rise to walk to the woods at Christmas. He and Maggie go together to the city to a comfortable home for the aged. When I can, I go back to see them and Maggie gives my little boy the same peppermints she gave to me, and Lon points to my picture at his bedside and says I am doing "wonderful well."

Then one year, just as though he were talking of rabbits and snares, he smiles and says, "If I don't see you, dear, you remember I'm okay. If God wants me tomorrow I'm just as ready as I can be."

Soon—too soon—it happens. A hasty note comes saying Maggie is gone and I know it will not be long for him. Then sixteen days later he slips away and with him goes something of myself too precious to part with.

That is why, when Christmas comes, I search the snow, as if to see again the footprints of a pilgrim showing a child the way to heaven.

Mi'kmaq Memories

Annie Battiste

Home for Harriet and John Lewis [Annie's Battiste's parents] was a little house, a shell that was built by the money provided by the Indian agent. Most people got a shell. But from profits from their baskets, John and Harriet bought sheet rock and hired a Frenchman to finish their house. They had hardwood floors and an oilcloth flooring in the kitchen. They had two bedrooms upstairs and a kitchen and living room downstairs. These houses were not big, but they often had to hold a lot of people, especially during the annual *Pestie'wa'taqtimk*. This was the occasion for feasting and feting with friends and family.

Pestie'wa'taqtimk started on *Noelimk* or Christmas Day. The preparations for the event had gone on for a least a month or two before that. Food was gathered and stored and readied for the thirteen days of feasting and the all-night dancing at each of the little houses in the Mi'kmaw village. Each consecutive night, a different person's name was honoured. As each name was honoured the people would gather and then walk to the house singing Christmas carols or talking.

As they approached the house, a gun shot would announce their arrival. The host would open the door and invite them to enter. When they entered the house the leader of the procession gave the host a shaved wooden cross and a medal or tie or cloth wrapped around the cross. After asking the host if they might dance, they danced the traditional *ko'jua* dance around the stove until the house rocked to the rhythm. A loud "*Ta ho!*" would end the dance and they would then eat the meal prepared by the host.

When they had eaten and visited with the family, they then would start out to the next house and continue throughout the night until all the names for that night had been honoured.

My mother remembers these days fondly as they were a fun time for the people. They feasted and frolicked every night for thirteen nights until the last day, January 6.

This last night of *Pestie'wa'taqtimk* festivities commemorated the three kings' arrival at the manger bearing gifts for the Baby Jesus. On this last night there was a square dance and people would come and dance all evening. A king and queen would be selected previously to host the evening's dance, and they would come dressed in a king and queen's costume.

A Memory of Ironville

Fr. Rod MacSween

When I was past middle age, I learned a startling bit of family history. I have already related the origin of the name Ironville: there were iron ore deposits beneath the soil of our farm. The government had done some exploratory work and then desisted. In leaving the area, the officials explained that they were retaining a fifty-foot driveway up to the mines on the edge of my grandfather's property. This fifty-foot driveway extended all the way up to the hinterland of the farm and was in actual fact a part of the farm. It could be used but it could not be owned.

The years passed by and the dubious nature of my grandfather's title to that driveway was forgotten. Then the blow fell.

The neighbour who owned the next farm remembered how the driveway slumbered like a wild animal ready to be seized by the first claimant. He reasoned that it belonged to the first man who claimed it, not to the man who had managed, apparently who had owned, it in the past. He went to the county clerk, paid some kind of tax, and the land was his, at least on paper.

My grandfather must have been completely stunned by the news when it came. Nothing of that sort had been envisaged. The land was behind his fence, he and his father had cultivated it, they had walked over it often. How could it be anyone else's?

As he engaged a lawyer and fought for his land, the farm went steadily downhill. Cattle and lambs were sold to pay the lawyer and the grandfather saw his hard work going for nothing. Finally it was decided that the driveway was his, but a hard price had been paid, and ill will was a permanent ingredient in the air. The two families were like tiny armies waiting for open warfare to break out. It seemed that they were present at the beginning of one of those famous rural feuds which start with violence and end up in myth and legend.

That year, at Midnight Mass, the parish priest spoke of the peace that Christ brought to earth, and he ended by saying that two families in the parish were behaving as enemies and that they should come together during the Christmas season. That day, after their Christmas meal, my grandfather declared that he was going over to the neighbours' house and he wanted his brother—Uncle Mick whom I dimly remember—to come with him. They spent some time putting on their heavy winter clothing and, while they were thus engaged, the door opened and the neighbour appeared.

He fell on his knees before my grandfather and begged his pardon, admitting that he himself was totally to blame. My grandfather raised him to his feet and forgave him. Then followed a time of laughing and rejoicing in which (almost) all joined. When the neighbours had left amid a chorus of good wishes, all agreed that he was an innocent "who did not know what he was doing" and that he was a good man at heart.

But then spoke up the great Dissenter, my father, at that

time (I guess) about twelve years of age. "He knew what he was doing. He was old enough to know. Nobody can tell me that he did not know!"

I don't know how he was answered. I'm sure that any attempt to change him would have ended in failure. There was a streak in him of uncompromising honesty that refused to be deterred by fear or be confused by sophistry. This streak must have caused difficulty, but because of it I was always proud of him.

Many years later, I found myself in conversation with a slender white-haired man of about sixty years of age. He said he was originally from Boisdale and his name was MacMullin. He was the father of Mrs. Effie Duggan, the Heights. "Did you know my father . . . ?"

"I was walking along the railroad as we used to do in those days, when I saw your father coming towards me. You know, we never passed anyone without stopping to chat. It would have been an insult to simply walk by."

"And what did you chat about?" I asked.

He said, "He had a dollar bill in his hand and he showed it to me. He said that he had found it on the road and he was taking it to the parish priest who would announce the finding on Sunday."

He looked at me knowingly, proud of his little anecdote. And I was proud too, proud of that streak in my father that may have made him difficult but that certainly made him honourable and admired.

Christmas on Long Island

Mary Sarah MacNeil

Oh yes, Christmas—we'd hang up our stockings. We wouldn't go to Midnight Mass or anything because we had no way of getting to church. But we'd hang up our stockings and put decorations up, and put a little tree up, and the paper around cigarettes—well, we didn't have cigarettes, but the paper around tea, the aluminum foil around the tea, roll it up in balls, put it here and there in the tree. Cut it in small, small strings and tie that to the tree so you'd have some tinsel on the tree.

We used to have to go to bed early. And our uncle, he used to butcher a cow before Christmas. And he would go out and get the cow's foot. He'd stay in the path, and he'd put the cow's foot tracks here and there.

Then he'd get the broom and make skips. So we'd think it was Santa Claus's reindeer that came down the skips, where the broom was, where the sleigh went, skipped through.

And we had a brake in the flue, by the way Santa Claus was coming down, coming out through the brake. And we have our stockings hanging there.

My uncle'd take the brake out of the flue in the nighttime, sprinkle some soot out around.

We'd get up in the morning, "Oh, my God, look at the mess Santa made last night!"

We'd leave a little lunch for him. They'd drink the glass of milk—they'd drink half the glass of milk, and they'd eat half a cookie, and, "Oh, my God, he was in a hurry last night—he only had half the cookie!"

Oh, Christmas was real. Because we had no TV—there was no such thing as two Santa Clauses. Only the one Santa Claus.

Fighting for the Light

Capt. Michael Tobin

I was going to write a story for *The Downhomer*—that's a magazine for Newfoundlanders living away. That's when they were going to take the light and the horn, off of Jude Island.

When we left Argentia, Newfoundland, there was ten or twelve policemen come aboard. We didn't know where they were going. [*Mr. Tobin was Captain of the Newfoundland coastal ferries at this time.*] And when we got to Great Paradise on our regular run, a motorboat come after, a large motorboat, and thirty-five carpenters. They all come aboard and we went on and we did our other ports until we got up to Little Harbour West, I think it was. And then, we went out to Jude Island. There was only a couple of people living there.

Anyway, when we got out there, we anchored off about half a mile and we went ashore with the policemen in the boat. We didn't know what they were doing. When we got in the beach, here was the ladder going up to the lighthouse—God, maybe seventy or eighty feet—and there was three men in every step on the way up with loaded muskets.

And one Sgt. Whalen got out of the boat in the beach and they called out to him to go back. Get back in the boat. "If you walk up over that beach, you'll have to be carried back." And a blaze of fire come out towards us. I don't think they had bullets there, but the powder. Those big (muskets), you know, about five feet long. There was a streak of fire coming out in our direction.

And they told him if he walked up over that beach he'd be shot.

So, policemen didn't have guns. We never did, haven't got them today. [*This was 1998*]. So anyhow, he got back in the boat.

And by this time there was about a hundred boats and dories and motorboats blocked us in and we couldn't get out. We were in this little cove under the lighthouse. What they were going to do—they were going to take the lighthouse down—or the horn down out of it—and put it on St. Jack's Island. And there was a couple of men—two of them were from my home—were drowned right there. There's a cross on the rock right under where we were landing. At Jude Island. And they told the police that. They said, "There's bodies drifting around there yet under those rocks. If the horn was there then it wouldn't have happened."

So anyhow, after a while we persuaded him that the police would go back to the ship and there would be no more trouble. They let us out. We rowed the policemen aboard and we went back to Paradise and landed the carpenters and landed the police and landed the skip—then went on our run.

And the horn was left, it's there today.

Now I was told that the father and son were there—and one other man—they were coming from St. John's for Christmas after buying their winter supplies. And they ran ashore. And they got on this rock where the sea beat up the little boat. But the son sat on the rock—there was only enough space at high water just to sit there—and he held the father with one hand and he held the other man, Mr. Sparrow, with the other hand, until both of them died. Then he let them go.

He was rescued the next day and he went to the States after that and he never came back. I don't know what happened to him. He was the son.

They got the father, they got his body—but they never got Mr. Sparrow. And one of the fellows forbidding police to come ashore—he told him that day there that those bodies are drifting around there yet, that's why the cross is on the rock. That's where the young fellow sat when he held his father till he died. (*And he felt that if there'd been a horn. . . .*) Oh yes, they wouldn't have made in there, they'd have heard it.

And then they put the horn there after that. But now they wanted to take it out of there and bring it up to St. Jack's Island because there was people were moving off of Jude. (*But the community did not permit it.*) No, they never allowed it. They told him that day. They stayed there, I think—someone told me they stayed there a couple of days after we left to make sure there'd be nobody come back. Oh yes. There was no way they could ever get that horn out of it. You know, there'd be a war.

When They Arrested Santa Claus

Johnny Abbass

I have a picture of my brother George with the Santa Claus outfit on.

Well, what we used to do, about a week before Christmas. He'd get dressed up as Santa Claus. I'd take him around. We'd have a bag with gifts in it from Santa Claus. We'd drop into the different stores uptown. We'd see the manager—and I'd say, "Come on over and say hello to Santa Claus." The guy'd, you know, get really—they wouldn't know who Santa Claus was. They'd ask me, "Who is it?" I said, "What do you mean, asking who it is? That's Santa Claus! You don't ask who he is. Can't you tell?" Said, "Gee whiz."

So anyway. This evening I had him up on Charlotte Street.

And we were driving down Charlotte Street. And the policeman was directing traffic there at Pitt and Charlotte. So he had the traffic stopped. So I made a right turn on Pitt Street. He blew the whistle and came after me. He'd been directing the traffic up Pitt Street, and turning left. Well, I didn't think there was any problem, me turning right on Pitt Street, off of Charlotte.

So he came over and he stopped me. He said, "Who do you think you are?" He said, "Didn't you see me directing traffic there?" I said, "Look," I said, "you were pulling the traffic down Charlotte Street from your left." I said, "All we did was make a right turn." And with that, my brother George got mad. The policeman said, "Who the hell are you!" I said to George, "Hey, be quiet, Santa Claus."

So he turned around, and he made us go down to the police station. And he issued a ticket at the police station. And he asked me, "What's your name?" I said, "My name is Johnny Abbass." He said, "What's your name?" "Santa Claus." He said, "Give us your name!"

I said, "What do you mean, 'your name'?" I said, "Don't you know Santa Claus?"

So he's pointing his finger at Santa Claus, and I took a picture of that. They ran it in the paper the next day. They wanted to put it on the Canadian Press and I wouldn't let them. I mean, "Sydney Police Arrest Santa Claus"!

So we had to go to court. So we were told to be in court next Saturday. That's two weeks before Christmas. So I turn around, and I go to court. Santa Claus comes with me—dressed up in his Santa Claus outfit. And the judge is there, and he says to the lawyer, he says, "Look," he says, "those fellows are making a joke of this trial."

So my uncle, the lawyer, he came to me and he said, "The judge is not very pleased." I said, "Why?" He said, "You're making a joke of this trial."

I said, "How are we? They arrested Santa Claus, didn't they?

Didn't they give the ticket to him?" I said, "Now, they've got the gall to give a ticket to someone who's out parading as Santa Claus, then that's who they're going to have to try."

The judge said, "Sorry," he says, "I have to postpone the hearing." He said, "When can you come back?"

To the lawyer, I said, "You tell him he has to hear the case right now"—this was three days before Christmas—"or," I said, "we want the case postponed till December the 14th next year. Because immediately after December 25th, Santa Claus is going back to the North Pole and he won't be returning till the 14th of December."

And you know what the judge said? He said, "Look," he said, "if you ever try this again. . . ." Oh, he was pretty upset.

So he dismissed the case.

Now, if they arrested you as Santa Claus, would you come as anybody else, to be tried?

Christmas Without Dickens

Hugh MacLennan

Time moves in spirals; each year the Victorian Age goes farther away and some of the earlier centuries draw near. The other day I found myself wondering what Christmas was like before Dickens invented the modern pattern, and I wondered if I would have felt more natural on a December 25th before Dickens' time than I do now.

For the past hundred years Christmas has meant turkey and plum pudding, nuts, candles, crackers and children's faces in the early morning. It is right and wonderful that this should be so. I wish all my Christmases had been Dickensian ones but for me the normal Christmas is unusual. When I was younger I used to feel badly about it. Yet in a strange way Christmas has been the greatest single day of the year for me. At least one of them changed my life.

The break in the normal pattern began for me long ago in the old war. On Christmas Eve in 1915 my father's unit was suddenly ordered to sail from Canada and the port was our own home town. On that Christmas Eve we stood on a street corner in a cold wind and watched the column of soldiers thump down the street in the darkness to the dock.

When they had passed from sight we went home to a house that had never seemed so cold. The next day, Christmas Day, fog came in from the ocean and we heard the ship's horn booming somewhere in the harbour, and I knew my father was still near and that the ship had not yet cleared port. I walked down the street past the decorations in other people's houses all the way to the park at the end of the city and there the trees were dripping with fog and there was a rime of ice on the rocks of the shore. Standing on the shore, slipping occasionally on the ice, I could see nothing but frigid salt water lapping in out of the fog that hid the ship and everything else. I did not stay long. On my way home I met people in the streets but hardly saw them. I wished someone would take the decorations from the doors and burn them. It was ten times worse that a day like this should be Christmas Day.

But that night friends came into the house after dinner and somehow (I don't know why, but a child's imagination is capable of almost anything) as I sat in the corner I seemed to witness the entire Christmas story as though I were there. The hills on which the shepherds watched their flocks were the hills about Halifax. The star was the bright Dog Star that had blazed in the sky the night before the fog came in, and the Child was every child that had ever been born. God knows all about it, I thought, and I felt sorry for Him because He did know, for that meant He knew how frightened people were and all about the war and the submarines under the water with the sailors in them pretending to be merry for the sake of Christmas while an officer squinted through the periscope to see if there were any ships on the horizon he might stalk and sink. I thought of the three kings walking very slowly beside their camels because they wanted to be kind to their beasts on a day like this, and finally of the Child in the manger feeling comfortable in spite of Herod and all the frightful things that were going to happen to Him when He grew up. A feeling of relief, the kind of pure happiness that arises only out of loneliness or despair, entered the house like a presence. That night I went to bed sure that somehow everything was going to turn out all right. It was this hope, I suppose, that the medieval painters found when they created their strangely primitive pictures of the Nativity. The hope, if not the belief, that love can be stronger than fear and that no matter what happens men will survive so long as they can continue to hope and think of someone beside themselves. Handel found something akin to this in passages of *The Messiah.* This hope has nothing whatever to do with the joviality of a modern Christmas. It is more primitive, more fundamental, less kindly and sometimes a little desperate. To many people Christmas meant this kind of hope before Dickens.

Another Christmas I remember vividly was the second during my three years at Oxford. In those days all my vacations were spent alone on the Continent and I found it a good idea to pick Christmas Day for travelling. Otherwise there was nothing to do but sit idle in a hotel room and eat meals in restaurants where the diners were half-ashamed to look at each other because their mere presence in a restaurant on Christmas Day proclaimed that they had no better place to go. So, this year, I found myself on a train passing out of Switzerland through the mountains of the Engadine into Italy.

The only concession I had made to Christmas was to buy

myself a second-class ticket. I rode on grey felt instead of the varnished boards of third-class. The train stopped in St. Moritz early in the morning and in the bright sunlight I saw the red sleighs of the winter-sports hotels and even caught sight of an English student I knew who was there for the skiing. The door of my compartment was thrown open by a porter who lifted four pieces of luggage onto the rack and went out. The luggage was of the grain-leather variety that was popular with well-heeled travellers before the days of air transport. A man and a woman followed the luggage into the compartment and sat down. The woman was in furs and the man wore one of those coats with astrakhan collars that made European business men look like diplomats and diplomats look like Russian conspirators. The only attention I paid them at first was to regret that they were there at all.

I had been up late the night before, I had a mild hangover and I needed sleep badly. With the compartment alone to myself I could have stretched out full-length on the seat. Now I crouched in the corner by the window and waited for the train to start. Presently it gave a jerk and moved out of the station. I saw the horses with their bright red plumes nodding gaily as they pulled newly-arrived guests up the slopes to the hotels; the frozen lake appeared with mist flashing above it.

And in the bright sunshine of a clear morning Mount Corveglia looked as perfect and as unreal as any Alp I have ever seen in a picture postcard. Then as the train began to pull solidly up the Bernina Pass, each thrust of the connecting rods communicating itself to the broad of my back, I closed my eyes and fell asleep.

When I woke there was no sunlight and the land outside the window was bare, steep and white with an utter absence of life that appears in very high mountains above the timber line in winter. The train wound up the pass which would ultimately lead it down into Italy. We entered a cloud and discovered it was a snowstorm. Once the cloud parted and a mountain appeared like a crude isosceles triangle, but the snow closed in again and again there was nothing to see.

We stopped at a little place called Bernina Hospiz and after the train got under way again a new guard opened the door and asked to see our tickets. I asked him in German if the train was on time and he answered in German that it was only a few minutes late. The man who had worn the astrakhan coat said something to him in Italian, then the door closed and we were alone as only strangers can be in the compartment of an international train in Europe. "So this is Christmas!" I thought, and closed my eyes.

Sleep was impossible now, so I gave up and took a book from my bag and began to read. The man and the woman said little to each other. He sat like a statue with his arms folded and his head on the back of the seat; she sat with her hands in her lap and her small, cleanly-cut face expressive of nothing but tension.

The man, I thought, would produce tension in almost anyone. I guessed him to be about fifty, which in those days seemed a great age to me, and for a while I thought he must be an officer on leave from a European army. He had a lean face with a scar on his left cheek and a thin, determined mouth.

The scar gave me the idea that he might be a German until I noticed that it was a jagged one. No duelling sword, but probably a chunk of red-hot metal blown from the casing of a shell, had made that welt. I doubted if he was an Italian, then decided he was probably a Pole.

The woman was much younger, so much younger she could have passed for his daughter were it not obvious from their manner that she was nothing of the kind. Now and then he looked at her, his eyes glanced off then returned. Her figure was slim and she was fashionably dressed, and her face called my eyes back to her, too. It held a strange blend of wantonness and innocence. I doubted if she was a day over twenty-five.

The man closed his eyes and gently massaged them and when his eyes were obscured by his fingers he looked old and tired.

When he opened them again they flinched in the hard light and at last he said something loud enough for me to hear it.

"What day is it?"

Without much expression she said, "Don't you really know?"

"Oh," he said and his face changed. "So it's Christmas. Ever since I got up I've been thinking Christmas was tomorrow even though I knew all along it was today."

The man was not a European at all. The accent was pure Bostonian and immediately I became curious. How could any New Englander look as European as this man?

"What's Christmas like in Hungary?" he said.

"When my father was alive it was a great feast. Boars were roasted for the peasants and everyone was happy. It was not like these hotels. It was not. . . ."

"For God's sake don't cry," he interrupted. "I can't stand women who cry."

I felt like an eavesdropper. They had heard me speak German to the guard and obviously they took it for granted that I knew no English, for any European student who knew even a few sentences would have shown off to the guard of a Swiss train.

"Just tell me this," the man went on in his Boston accent, "why do you want to marry a man as old as your father?"

"Because you remind me of him."

"He was a Hungarian baron and I'm an American. Why don't you fall in love with someone your own age?"

"If you did not want me to love you, why did you begin by making love to me?"

"Oh, God!" he said.

"What is a young man? What has he done? A young man is nothing at all. And since the war I find all the young men barbarous."

I looked very hard at my book but I was unable to follow a sentence in it. I looked out of the window and there was nothing but the driving snow, and still there was the steady push, push, push of engine-thrusts against my back We were not yet at the top of the pass. I glanced round again and the two were looking at each other. The man's stern face had become soft, gentle and full of pain. He was leaning forward, oblivious of my presence, one hand on the girl's knee.

"Listen, my dear, and I will tell you something sentimental. Where I come from the best time of the year seems to be the autumn. I said seems to be. Autumn is the late middle age of the year and of course very interesting. Behind my father's house there used to be one of the tallest maple trees in the county, and in early October it was something to look at. In that season of the year—the French call it *Toussaints*—the air is so still you can hear butternuts strike the ground a hundred yards away. That was when our maple was magnificent. It was like a tower of flame. But every year the wind came and ripped it apart. Next day the tree was as bare as a scarecrow."

She looked at him. "What difference does it make? I love you."

"Oh, go to hell!" he said. She got up abruptly and left the compartment. I thought she was on her way to the ladies' room, but almost at once I heard the door of the next compartment open and close and knew she had gone into it to be away from the man. He swallowed hard, took out his handkerchief and blew his nose. For nearly a minute he tried to sit still as though nothing had happened. Then he seemed to recollect where he was and I became uncomfortably conscious of his eyes on my profile. I pretended to be concentrating on my book and to make it seem real I even turned a page. Then I heard his voice speaking to me in German.

"You are a student?"

I looked up. "Yes."

"Speak English?"

"No," I lied.

"I guessed you didn't."

He took out a gold cigarette case, snapped it open and passed it over. I took one and when I saw he did not intend to smoke I lit up and leaned back.

"I'm an American," he said. "There are some people who just can't live in the States and I'm one of them. I felt I was suffocating. Do you know what I mean?"

My German was adequate for the monosyllabic answers which were all he required. At that time I could understand far better than I could speak.

"When the war began I couldn't get out soon enough. I left my wife"—his face twisted slightly—"and came over and joined the French Army. I got hell knocked out of me. One lung and this." He tapped the scar on his cheek. "I guess I got to thinking like a European. Anyway my wife divorced me when I wouldn't come home."

I could think of no reply, and in the silence I became aware that the pulse from the engine had changed. The push, push, push against my back had almost ceased and the train seemed to be running faster and smoother. I glanced out of the window but could still see nothing.

"I suppose we've reached the top of the pass," I said.

He glanced out automatically, then said, "Funny way to spend Christmas. It's the one day when I feel an outcast in Europe. It's the one day I remember what it was like when I was a nice little boy with a nice New England conscience and didn't know one damned thing about anything."

I felt his eyes appraising me and wished he wouldn't look at me like that. It is something an older man should never do to a youth because it takes an unfair advantage of him.

"Well," he said, "and what did you think of the lady?"

I must have blushed for he recalled his manners and apologized. But he went on talking. "I just told her to go to hell. Do you know why? Because I love her. She's been having around hotels for two years with any man who'll pay her bills and I still love her. Do you know why? Because I'm practically an old man and she's young, and I'm damned if I ever want to see the day when I'm pitied."

He glanced at his watch and muttered something, then went out into the corridor and came back minutes later.

"The guard says we'll be half an hour late in Milan. This damned day!"

Then he went into the next compartment and I tried to keep my mind on my book. It was one of my curious Christmas Days.

After I came back from Oxford the unnatural pattern went on. Instead of being a day of joy, Christmas became a day of insight and experience. Sometimes I was in New York, sometimes at home where it was normal enough. But generally something happened and once—the most wonderful Christmas I ever spent—life seemed desperate before suddenly it changed. That was the one I spent in the hospital wondering whether my wife would live or die. That was the Christmas when I never thought of Dickens at all, but went back into time about as far as a man can ever go.

The struggle had been going on for days, each day harder than the one before. It was a fair Christmas, but I entered it with a foreboding I have never known before or since. Strain and imagination were telling. Everyone I passed, even beautiful girls, I seemed to be seeing as though they were old, their flesh shrunken as in the hour of their death. Sunlight flickered among the tree boles on the mountain and squirrels came down through fluffy snow to the hospital doors. A church carillon in the lower City was playing "Adeste, Fideles" and the faithful were coming from early Mass. I went into the hospital and the nurse's whisper was not reassuring. In the room I met with bare recognition. It was the same sight that had become so familiar: the tubes, the bottle dripping its liquid into the splinted arm, the rattle of desperate breathing.

I sat down and time ticked on, empty and without significance. Some time around noon the nurses got me out of there and I sat in the lounge at the end of the floor and looked down at the city in the sun and snow. Christmas dinner was brought but I ate only a few bites and pushed the plate away. I was the only person around until an interne came in and sat down and talked.

I was grateful for his thoughtfulness in sitting with me that afternoon instead of going home. After a time I left him and went back into the room. From a radio in the room next door came a faint sound of carols and I thought I could hear the story of the Nativity being retold. Perhaps I slept. Those days I hardly knew when I was asleep or awake, but all the time I was conscious of the desperate struggle for breath on the bed. I remember noticing it was dark in the room and that lights had come on outside. It was as dark, I thought, as eternity; as the low bottom of an anaesthetic; as the beginnings of time.

Then suddenly I sat upright with the feeling that something had brushed me lightly and passed. Now, though everything was the same even to the sound of the breathing, the room felt different and an enormous pressure slid away and seemed to sink into the floor.

I went over to the bed, then turned as I felt a hand on my shoulder and saw the doctor's face.

"You'd better stay here tonight," he said.

It would have sounded worse than strange, it would have been wrong and shocking if I had said to him, who had the responsibility, that a few minutes before he entered the room I had felt death go out of it and life come back in.

That night I walked down the steep hill to Sherbrooke Street and when I got on the bus everyone looked young and their faces shone. A friend had asked me to a Christmas party and I looked in for a while but did not stay, for it was a Dickens party and the longer I stayed the more surely I felt like the skeleton at a Roman feast. I walked home and went to bed without dinner and as I fell asleep Handel's music sang through my mind—that exultant chorus that seems to express all the passionate hope of the human race—"O thou, that tellest good tidings to Zion—arise and shine, for thy light is come!"

The next day, as I knew would be the case, the doctor stopped worrying, too.

Beannachdan na Nollaig Oirbh!

Mickey Bean Nilag MacNeil
(Migi Mac Bean Nìlleig Ruairidh Eòin a' Phlant)

Uair dhen t-saoghal, an toiseach . . . tha mi 'creidsinn fhathast, ma dh'fhaoidte aréir na h-eaglais, gu bheil e ann (Latha nan Trì Rìghean). Ach Latha nan Trì Rìghean: chanadh 'ad sin ris an Nollaig Mhór, ged nach eil uiread sin 'ga thoirt dha an diugh, air tàilleabh gum biodh an Nollaig againn as deaghaidh Feasgar nam Bonnach—air a' cheathreamh làtha air fhichead, agus Latha Nollaig air a' chóigeamh latha air fhichead dhen a' mhìos. Na trì rìghean . . . bha a' latha sin an tacsa ris an Nollaig Mhóir.

Uell, an nuair sin Latha na Nollaig gu Latha nan Trì Righean . . . dà là dheug as deaghaidh na Nollaig a bha Latha nan Trì Rìghean. Siod agad a' latha a chaidh na rìghean gu stabull, aréir a' bhiobaill, aig an àm a thàinig Crìosda do 'n talamh. 'S e na trì rìghean a chaidh 'ga choimhead 's a thug na preasain uige. Bha sin na bu mhotha an uair sin 'na latha eil' a thànaig air an t-saoghal—na h-uaislean móra sin a' dol 'ga choimhead. Sin agad ceann na Nollaig mar a chanadh 'ad.

A-nist, bhiodh feadhainn dhe na seann daoine . . . bhiodh 'ad

a' deanamh deisealachd airson seo, airson a' latha fa dheireadh.
Feadhainn dhe na seann daoine, anns a' mhìos November—null
a' sin, bhiodh 'ad a' gearradh connadh, 's a' spleatadh connadh,
a' cuir connadh mu seach, 'ga tharraing astaigh 's deanamh a
h-uile sgàth cho math's a b'urrainn dhaibh deiseil airson nuair a
thigeadh an Nollaig nach biodh aca ri sgàth dhèanamh gus an
déidh Latha nan Trì Rìghean. Bha connadh gu leòir ac' astaigh.
Cha robh cion-connaidh air an teine. Uell anist, bha bucaidean do
dh'uiste ri 'n taobh. Dh'fhaodadh 'ad beòthaichean a bhiadhadh 's
beòthaichean a bhleoghainn. Cha robh 'ad a' dol amach a dh'obair.
Cha robh obair ann. Cha robh ann ach an tuathanchas. Bha biadh
gu leòir aca 's an t-seilear, 's biadh gu leòir ac' a ghabhail. Dé an
còrr a bhiodh dhìth orra?

Ged a shaoileas sinn an dràst' nach robh 'ad anns na h-
àmannan sin cho math dheth 's tha sinn-ne, 's ann a bha 'ad na
b'fheàrr dheth. Cha robh cùram idir orr'. Bha t'airgead 's do
bhiadh a' tionnadh astaigh ugad 's tu 'cadal air tàilleabh gu robh
na beòthaichean a's an t-sabhal agus a' mhuc a thogadh tu 'fàs
reamhar. 'S e an cùram a tha 'gad mhilleadh. An diugh, cha n-eil
e gu deifir co-dhiubh gu bheil thu 'nad mhaighstir-sgoil no gu
bheil thu 'nad dhotair; tha thu an greim.

Bha 'ad a' deanamh deiseil a dhol dha 'n aifreann Feasgar
nam Bonnach. Anist an toiseach, cha bhitheadh 'ad a' dol a ghabhail comuinn air an Nollaig idir. Corra-dhuin' a bhiodh a' dol
a ghabhail comuinn, ach cha bhiodh an uiread a' dol a ghabhail
comuinn. Uaireannan, thadhladh 'ad 's dhannsadh 'ad air Feasgar
nam Bonnach—dhannsadh.

Ach an toiseach anist, anns na h-àiteachan seo, cha robh
eaglais againn idir. Dh'fheumamaid a dhol anull gu Eaglais
Eilean na Nollaig. Bhiodh 'ad a' fàgail tràth feasgar no 'n déigh
meadhon làtha. Dh'fhuiricheadh 'ad thall a's na taighean. Bhiodh
rud ac' a dh'òladh 'ad 's dhannsadh 'ad. Startadh 'ad dhachaidh.
Uell, bhiodh aca ri coiseachd, mar gum b'eadh, coiseachd dha
'n Mhaise. Uell, an fheadhainn a bha 'fuireach ach goirid air

an taobh seo—cha robh e cho dona. Ach feadhainn a bhiodh amuigh againn-ne (muinntir a' Chùil Bhig), bha pìos ann. Ach cha chuireadh e sìon orra! Bhiodh òrain aca 's bhiodh 'ad gu math sunndach, toilichte.

Bhiodh an t-suipear aca nuair a thigeadh 'ad dhachaidh on aifreann. Bha feòil-cruidh, feòil-muiceadh aca. Bhiodh 'ad a' marbhadh caoraich, uain, 's bhiodh maragan aca; bhiodh gach seòrsa. Bhiodh bòrd dha rìreabh ann! Bha am biadh seo 'ga dhèanamh aca fhéin. Cha n-e biadh-stòir mar a gheibh thu an dràst' 'ga thoirt dhachaidh. Agus bha e 'na bhiadh nach itheadh 'ad a h-uile làtha. Agus creid thusa gun còrdadh gearraidhean do dheagh aran milis leotha.

Boxing Day 's Christmas trees . . . cha robh an leithid sin ann. 'S e na stòraichean a thug sin amach.

Christmas Greetings

At one time, in the beginning . . . I think it's still the case, perhaps, according to the church, that it's still that way (the Day of the Three Kings is celebrated). But the Day of the Three Kings, they called that The Great Christmas, although it isn't observed to that extent today. We kept Christmas after the Evening of the Bannocks, on the 24th of the month, and Christmas Day on the 25th. The three kings . . . that day was part of The Great Christmas. Well, at that time there was Christmas Day to the Day of the Three Kings. The Day of the Three Kings was twelve days after the Christmas day.

There you have it, the day that the kings went to the stable, according to the bible, when Jesus was born. The three kings are the ones who went to see him and gave him presents. That was a day greater than any other the world had seen—those distinguished gentlemen travelling to see Jesus. There you have it, the end of Christmas as they used to say.

Now, some of the old people would . . . they would prepare for this—for the last day. Some of the old-timers, around November, would cut and split firewood, haul it in and store it and set everything up as well as they could, so that when Christmas came they wouldn't have a thing to do until after the Day of the Three Kings. There was lots of firewood put by. The fire didn't lack for fuel. Well now, there were buckets of water on hand. They could feed and milk the cows. They weren't going off to jobs. There weren't any jobs. There was nothing but farming the land.

There was plenty of food in the cellar and lots to eat. What more could they want? Though we think in these times we are so well off, they had the best of it. They had no worries. Your wealth and sustenance was turning over for you while you slept on account of the cows in the barn and the pig you raised getting fat. Worry is your ruination. Today, it doesn't matter if you're a doctor or a school teacher, you're cornered!

They got ready to go to mass on the Night of the Bannocks (Christmas Eve). Now at first, they wouldn't go to take the sacrament at Christmas at all. An occasional person would, but most didn't. Sometimes, they would visit and dance on the Night of the Bannocks—they would dance.

But at first, in these parts, we didn't have any church. We had to go across to the Christmas Island church. They used to leave early in the afternoon or after mid-day. They would stay over in houses, have something to drink, dance and start home. Well, they would have to walk, as it were, to Benacadie Pond. It wasn't so bad for nearby people on this side. Those of our folk (from the Rear) had to go some distance. But that didn't bother them the least little bit! They had songs and they were happy and in good cheer.

They would eat supper when they arrived home. There was beef and pork. They used to slaughter a sheep—a lamb—and they would have sausages. There was every kind. Indeed, the table was a banquet! It was homemade fare that they prepared themselves. It wasn't store food like you take home now, and it wasn't common everyday food. Believe you me; they were festive with lovely slices of sweet bread.

Boxing Day and Christmas trees . . . there was no such thing. It's the stores that brought that out.

Recorded, transcribed, and translated by Seumas Watson.

Archie Nathanson's Store on Christmas Eve

Paul MacDougall

One of my best high school pals, David MacDonald, asked me to spend the early part of Christmas Eve with our friend Sheldon Nathanson at Archie Nathanson's—their family-run store since the 1920s, located on Victoria Road, in Sydney's mini mighty United Nations district of Whitney Pier.

This was a few years before we were old enough to go to the Bonnie Prince Beverage Room to get the reputed two free Christmas Eve draught beers, yet were old enough to drive a car and stay out late. I had to be home in time to go to Midnight Mass at St. Theresa's Church and then be back home to open presents with my Mom, Dad and brother.

David and I headed down to the Pier in his father's car around eight on Christmas Eve, 1976. There were two women working at that hour. Barbara Nathanson still affectionately calls them "the girls" and swears that they were the heart and soul of the store. "Everybody knew them and they knew everybody."

Countless folks from the Pier as well as people from "over town" and other neighbouring communities, especially New

Waterford, would shop at Archie's. "The King of Lower Prices" stretched pretty far back off the Victoria Road entrance and contained clothes for kids, youth, men and women, of every shape, size and description. Prices were always decent and were often discounted so people with large families could afford to clothe themselves in stuff that wasn't going to wear out.

Large families like the nine-children Doue family of the Pier. And it wasn't just that these families put off their Christmas shopping to the last minute; John Doue told me that shopping at Archie Nathanson's on December twenty-fourth had become a tradition. "My mother, sisters, brothers, cousin Brenda—we all went there." Coming in at the early evening hour was something they looked forward to. You came in with expectations of a fun time. You would meet with other families and wish them all Merry Christmas.

The girls' welcome greeting at the door was part of the store's appeal. But seeing two seventeen-year-old scraggly-looking guys wander in on Christmas Eve an hour before closing warranted a little closer scrutiny.

"We're here to see Sheldon."

"He's downstairs in Shoeland."

At either end of the store were stairs leading down to Shoe-land—the domain of Sheldon.

There was Sheldon towering at about six feet with a huge bushy head of hair, grinning from ear to ear as his Christmas Eve entertainment arrived. The wall behind this larger-than-life teenage businessman was covered with what looked like thousands of shoeboxes. "Archie Nathanson" was on the sign outside the store but so was the word "Shoeland" in big letters—a selection that could rival any warehouse at the North Pole.

Sheldon let us know, "We will be closing up at nine."

That was when our fun would begin, locked with your closest pals inside one of the coolest, oldest stores in town, with nothing to do but carry on as if you were in Santa's workshop.

The last few people in the store were just looking for tape or wrapping paper—after all, this was the only place open—every other store in Sydney had locked the doors at five, if not earlier.

Sheldon wished the ladies Merry Christmas and said he'd see them the day after Boxing Day when the store reopened. The only cars on the street now were there to pick up the ladies. A lone police car passed by. The odd taxi. Just a bit of snow was falling. Enough. Doors shut, locked. The place was our own.

"Here, take these," Sheldon said, handing us each a tiny flashlight. "I'll get the lights, you get downstairs." In the dark, David and I made it to the toy department to get prepared. The game was on.

The memory is still vivid. Archie's carried toy guns that emitted an amazing array of sparkles. The idea was to shoot with them in the dark, running and tearing up and down the stairs—a two-storey business with a set of stairs at either end—running in total darkness, with only a flashlight that you quickly turned off once you got your sparkle gun—creeping around, hiding under counters, crawling into counter drawers, awaiting your victim out there somewhere in search of you.

Call it cops and robbers, call it hide and seek, call it sparkle gun spotlight, call it what you want. I call it good times—good memories of good friends. And when the Pier cops rolled by around eleven and saw us coming out the door, they had the window down and one officer said to the other, "Nothing going on here. It's just Sheldon playing with the lights again."

We had cleaned up any mess, put away the toys, and left everything as it was. I made it to church on time; and Herman and Barbara Nathanson were none the wiser. Well, until now.

I should add that Herman was one of four men who started the Whitney Pier Christmas parade, which eventually moved into downtown Sydney. He helped bring the Welcome Wagon program to the Pier, and he held the longest running promotion on CJCB radio—the Baby Parade program.

Coming Home for Christmas—1943

Catherine MacIsaac McKenna

Preparing to come home to Port Hood at Christmas 1943 was very exciting for me. I had been in Halifax since 1941, working at CN Telegraph, but had not had sufficient time off at Christmas for the trip. The year before, I had very kindly been invited to Christmas dinner by Dr. and Mrs. Peter Smyth Campbell (parents of Bishop Colin Campbell) in Halifax.

In 1943 I was working in the Treasury Office of Eastern Air Command and had four days off—December 24, 25, 26 and 27—so was all set for the trip home by train.

We left Halifax at 6:30 a.m. and the Halifax CN Station was a bustling place indeed, with service people and civilians alike going home for Christmas. The day dawned bright and sunny but as we travelled on, the weather changed and it became very cloudy. By the time we arrived at Mulgrave we had a full-blown Maritime snowstorm. The train being so long because of extra Christmas travellers and Christmas mail, had to be divided in half, with each half requiring a separate ferry trip to Point Tupper. This of course was before the causeway was built.

After several hours involved in getting across the Strait of Canso, we arrived at Point Tupper and transferred to the Inverness train, better known as the Judique Flyer. Although a snowplow had already cleared the track to Inverness, during our long delay in getting across the Strait and boarding the Inverness train, the track was snowed in again. The plow operators were already in Inverness, thinking they had finished their day's work, but they had to return to Point Tupper and clear the track again ahead of the train. We had no choice but to sit on the train for another few hours and, by this time, many of the passengers were getting impatient with the delays. Some opened the bottles of "Christmas Cheer" which they were bringing home and the bottles were passed around the car for anyone who wanted a sip. There was singing and storytelling and that helped pass the time. The only Port Hood people I can now remember being on the train were Florence MacPhee and Angus D. MacDonald (John Colin's brother who was working as a carpenter in Halifax).

Finally we were on our way, following behind the plow for the usual stops at Port Hawkesbury, Port Hastings, Troy, Creignish, Craigmore, Long Point, Judique, Maryville, and arriving at Port Hood at 1:00 a.m.

My father, waiting for the train since 7:00 p.m. when it was due to arrive, had come to the station with Dougald J. MacDonald, the mail carrier, and we were to have a ride to the end of our road with him. When the mail was loaded onto the truck, it would not start—the gas line was frozen and the truck had to be left there. Fortunately, the MacPhees were there to meet Florence with the horse and wood sled and we all got a ride with them. As we passed St. Peter's Church, everyone was coming out of Midnight Mass—one of the main attractions of Christmas in Port Hood, and I had missed it.

It was still great to have been home for Christmas and the return trip to Halifax on December 27 was much more enjoyable with the trains running on time and we were already looking forward to coming home for Christmas the next year.

Christmas Tails

Maureen MacIntosh

It was Christmas Eve and a special one for me, the mother of two grown children. My daughter, who works in Toronto, was home for the Holidays and we were spending them with my son and daughter-in-law and their two dogs. Newman, the smaller dog, is a bit of a rogue, while Sawyer, the larger dog, is kind of a gentle nature.

Before we left for church and to visit relatives, a gift for each dog was taken from the large stash under the tree. Like children, they excitingly tore off the wrappings, and were very happy with gifts of pig's ears. As we left the house, we looked back at two contented dogs.

Upon returning home, around midnight, the dogs met us at the door and bolted outside. My son chose to stay out on this moonlit night and frolic with them for a while. My daughter-in-law was the first to enter the living room and a scream pierced the air. My daughter entered next and I heard her gasp. As I rounded the corner, I saw them standing knee deep in paper, cardboard and styrofoam particles. The dogs had opened every gift under the tree in hopes of finding another treat. Boxes of candy had the corners chewed, just to make sure of the contents, but the candy was intact. A crystal vase stood upright under the tree, its box and packing shredded about the room.

When my son entered, I can't repeat his first few words but he ended with, "Christmas is ruined!" Mother, in her wisdom, replied, "Christmas is a spirit that comes from the heart!"

We proceeded to dig out and exchange gifts and hug and

laugh till tears came. We couldn't identify the giver or receiver of some gifts. When the mess was cleared away, we changed into our comfy nightwear. As my son poured the wine, my daughter-in-law set out a scrumptious array of food and my daughter slipped *It's a Wonderful Life* into the VCR.

As I looked out onto the sparkling snow, I felt Jesus must have been born on a night as beautiful as this one and I realized that the true gifts of Christmas cannot be wrapped. They need to be exposed and shared with one another. We had been blessed with peace, love and goodwill on this special night.

These memories would be etched in our minds indelibly and bring forth joy and laughter in the days ahead.

Archie Neil Chisholm's Christmas Present

Mary Anne Ducharme

A great friend of anything Cape Breton, especially the music and the story-telling, Archie Neil Chisholm was stricken with polio early in life. As told in the biography *Archie Neil*, despite several strikes against him, he rose to become an essential element in Cape Breton Island life, a favourite Master of Ceremonies for outdoor concerts, and a CBC Radio broadcaster.

On Christmas Eve all the Chisholms, all except Momma and Archie Neil, went to Midnight Mass. Momma boiled a big pot of blue potatoes. And she also boiled two of the *isbean* in their casings, punching the sausages with a fork to let the air out. When the family got home, about two-thirty in the morning, the house was filled with spicy aromas and they had a big feed with huge slices of hot mince pie for dessert. They were happy enough, but it wasn't the same without Papa.

They had a tree decorated with dried cranberries and silver ornaments made from tea wrappers, ready for Santa Claus. T. Eaton's catalogue had a spring-wound cast iron train that moved on a track, and this was what Archie Neil wanted for Christmas. It cost $2.25. He knew it was unlikely he would get it, whether he was good or bad. He thought Santa Claus was a miserly old fraud, but tried to maintain a positive attitude, just in case.

He didn't get the toy train. What he did get was a pair of crutches carved by Peter Pat Coady. But he refused to try them while anyone was watching. When he did test them they felt clumsy; they hurt his armpits and wobbled, good for making him fall, he thought, and nothing else.

But Peter Pat came over one afternoon and he was a lot like Papa when he made up his mind.

"Don't put your weight on the armpits," he said, watching Archie Neil clump across the kitchen. The rest of the family had been banished from the room. "Those crosspieces can hold your weight. Use your hands and arms and shoulders. You're strong as an ox in the shoulders. Come on now, try it."

Peter Pat was right. But it still felt awkward. "Divide your weight between the crutches and your feet," he advised. "Then move the crutches ahead, swing your body, move the crutches, swing. You'll get the hang of it."

It worked! Archie Neil's heart suddenly raced with excitement. He was walking! Swinging back and forth across the kitchen.

"Now get me a nice cup of hot tea from the stove," Peter Pat said, "on your way by."

Archie Neil looked at him with disbelief.

"Next time," Peter Pat said, rumpling his hair.

"Yah," he answered, grinning. "Next time."

One Christmas Eve in the Korean War

Roly Soper

Whose idea it was we'll never know, nor would it much matter. It may have been the local commander of the Chinese Peoples Volunteers whose troops were facing and virtually encircling the Hook position. Probably not, because it was not the kind of thing a fighting soldier would squander his men on doing. More likely some propaganda people behind the lines made the plan. Anyhow, the very tired men in Lieutenant Peter Worthington's platoon in D Company of the 3rd Battalion, Princess Patricia's Canadian Light Infantry, were aghast just before daybreak to see silhouettes of what they thought were very large enemy soldiers, standing within pistol range of their fighting trench.

As eyes quickly adjusted with the gathering light, it was apparent they were gazing at Christmas trees, set there by stealthy soldiers. Good the enemy troops had not been sneaking in to attack, for they had come so close undetected.

In the brighter predawn the Patricias began to see leaflets, cards, letters hanging on the trees. With dawn's first true light they could see sparkles and glints. The enemy had hung little gifts on the trees, so they went over the top, though for certain enemy troops were watching with weapons poised.

Worthington's men grabbed up little glass animal figurines, greeting cards, scurried back to the fighting trench. It was a remarkable bonanza and spirits soared. But later, in even better light, they saw a couple of enemy soldiers and opened relentless fire on them, so the gesture had not interrupted their war.

Worthington later was advised that "intelligence" wanted all of the gift paraphernalia sent back through the echelons for analysis. He advised his men to keep the best for themselves and give up the rest. He still has some of the gifts in his home in Toronto.

The same day, Private Eddy Power had returned to C Company, which was out of the lines on rest. He had been on the staff of the NCO School, safe far behind the front lines, but he was a cutup and had done something that landed him back in a rifle company. Eddy came from the Glace Bay, Nova Scotia, area and was extremely well liked.

Somebody, either in the Princess Patricia's headquarters, but more likely back at 25th Canadian Infantry Brigade headquarters, thirty-five miles behind the lines, decided it would be good to set up Christmas trees at the enemy positions as well. One can see the toasty officers, well oiled with liquor, giggling about the lark in their mess. It was no secret that heavy drinking was rampant in such places.

Anyhow, poor Eddy Power, who a few days before had a cushy job near that very headquarters, was tapped for a Christmas Eve patrol. Sergeant Thomas Prince was in charge. He was the sniper sergeant for the Patricias battalion. Corporal Tommy Thompson, the Patricias sniper corporal, led the patrol. Tommy Prince had been wounded in the knee on the Hook less than two weeks before.

The soldiers toted out Christmas trees, set them up just yards from the enemy position and put safe conduct passes all around them. Just like the soldiers in Peter Worthington's platoon, the enemy did not cut Prince's men any slack.

As they withdrew, they put a barrage of mortar bombs onto them. It was a dark night, even though there was a half moon. There were thick snow clouds. The bombs burst around them and Thompson hustled them back to their home position.

All but one.

When they got into the fighting trench, the count was wrong. They waited awhile for Eddy Power to show up, then went back out to search for him.

They carried Eddy back in with them. Shrapnel from one of the bombs had struck him in the head.

At the Regimental Aid Post not far from the lines Lance Corporal Morehouse signed the identity certificate, based upon personally identifying Eddy's face. Sergeant Tommy Prince co-signed the certificate as the verifying officer in charge.

The time of death given on the certificate was 2335 hours—another twenty-five minutes and it would have been Christmas Day.

The duty driver who took Eddy's remains to the collection point in Yongdongpo on Christmas morning stopped at the Patricias A Echelon along the way. He parked his three-quarter-ton vehicle outside the cook tent, where the soldiers ate. He likely had coffee or breakfast.

Lance Corporal Walter Polkosnik from Edmonton was there. He went to the vehicle, lifted the canvas covering Eddy Power's body, felt great crushing sorrow for his friend.

At Yongdongpo they listed the clothing Eddy was wearing. He had nothing in his pockets, no rings, no personal effects. He had worn flannel pyjama pants beneath his woollen battle dress trousers, like all of his comrades, to stave off the cold.

In the cook tent at A Echelon, the cook was roasting turkeys for the Christmas dinner and fixing other delicacies that the small staff based there would enjoy. At around noon, the men entered the adjacent mess tent, sat at picnic tables. Lieutenant Colonel Herbert Wood, the Patricias commanding officer, came in with a cadre of headquarters officers. Some of them served the men, others did not. They sat with the men and picked away at the turkey dinner themselves.

Not a word was said about Eddy Power who had been sent to his death hours before to plant a Christmas tree in front of the enemy position. Not a word was said about any of the casualties, or about the war. The officers soon were gone, for they had many small units of the battalion to visit that day.

Eddy Power was buried in the U.S. Military Cemetery at Tanggok, now named the United Nations Memorial Cemetery, on December 29, at eleven o'clock in the morning. Like all others buried there during the war, his remains were wrapped in a square of tent canvas and bound with yellow field telephone wire.

A small bronze funereal bottle containing his burial records was put in the ground eighteen inches beneath the cross that marked his grave. The bottle is still there. The wooden cross was replaced long ago by a bronze grave marker that lies nearly flat to the ground. Eddy probably has become the soil of Korea.

One thing he was when he lived. He was the salt of the Earth! Though very young he looked very mature and as said, he was a cutup and very popular with others. On leave, and on excursions behind the lines, he would allege himself to be a fictitious soldier named Joe Dowey, Number SD1111.

When the Monument to Canadian Fallen was cast and set in place in the United Nations Cemetery in 2001, forty-nine years after his death, its base listed both Edward James Power and Joe Dowey.

Mabel Bell's Letters About Christmas

In 1890, Mabel Bell wrote to her mother-in-law Eliza Symonds Bell and her mother Gertrude McCurdy Hubbard from her and Alexander Graham Bell's home at Beinn Bhreagh, near Baddeck.

December 7th, 1890

My dear Mrs. Bell:

. . . We have decided to remain here over Christmas, as we think it better to do so on many accounts. . . . We are all so well here and Daisy is leading such a healthy happy outdoor life that we cannot bear to take her home and shut her up in the city. We feel also that by remaining over Christmas we can make the day a happy one to many poor people here to whom Christmas cheer has been unknown. We are going to have a Christmas tree for the children of our workmen, and try to make the day a pleasant one for them. We know all these people personally, which makes it a very different thing from dressing Christmas trees for utter strangers, which is the only way I could do anything of the kind for the poor in the city. . . .

December 11th, 1890

My darling Mother:

What will you say when I tell you that I have just come in from a walk with Alec beyond Elsie's house in a driving snow storm which obliterated our tracks almost as soon as made? . . .

It had just begun to snow when we left the house, and the trees were quite bare; as we returned there must have been nearly two inches of snow on the evergreen trees, and everything was perfectly beautiful. You will be surprised at my enthusiasm for the snow remembering how I used to hate it, but Beinn Bhreagh snow is a very different article from Washington or even Cambridge snow. There it is damp and chilly, a nuisance in every way; here it is dry and crisp and nice to walk in. . . .

I hope you don't think all this rhapsody is a prelude to telling you that we intend to stay here all winter! No indeed. I expect to be quite ready to go after Christmas, but I am more glad all the time that we have decided to remain.

You see Mamma darling, the knowledge that my husband thoroughly disapproved of all our present giving and receiving has spoilt my Christmases lately, and it seemed a shame to try to keep up a custom which was shutting out Alec from us and his children. There are enough other things which tend to keep him away. Yet I did not know how to stop it in Washington. I could not refuse to receive presents and it would have seemed mean not to give any. Here where it is impossible to send me presents, I can be excused from sending any either, and Alec can have his own way.

If you could see how happy he is now and how happy he is making the children and entertaining us all with his preparations for his Christmas pantomime to which all the work people's children are to be invited, I think you would admit we were acting for our best interests. Alec does not object to my giving presents if I chose at any other time, and that is what I am going to do, and isn't that better than hunting up and down Washington to find something I don't care very much about and which is only another thing for you to take care of simply because it is Christmas. I would so much rather save my money until I go to New York and see something I think really worthy of you.

I am going to send you a cheque for twenty-five dollars, fifteen for the Garfield Hospital and ten for the Children's, for Christmas cheer or anything you think best. . . .

Much love to you my darling Mamma.

Lovingly, Mabel

133

Cape Breton's Christmas

26 December, 1890

My darling Mamma:

We had a pleasant Christmas. It was bitterly cold, one of the coldest days we have had, and I feared the children from town at all events would not come, but they all did except one poor little town girl who got left by mistake and the poorest child of all, who was sick. Even the McCurdy babies came. . . .

We had about thirty children altogether, and I think they were very much pleased with the tree and with Alec's efforts for their entertainment. I know I saw my sewing class girls laugh and laugh with all their might and main for the first time in my acquaintance with them. We sent to Montreal for presents so all were provided with a little gift, a cornucopia of candy and a big red apple.

Today we harnessed the horses tandem to the sleigh and drove down over the beach to the little bridge and along the path to the houseboat and thence on the ice on which we traveled up the harbor and across the bay to carry the little sick girl's dolly to her. The dimples came in her face and she said she never had one before. . . .

We are going to light the tree again tomorrow for the workmen and their wives as one of them said he would walk miles to see such a sight and Alec is busy preparing for their entertainment so my letter is rather jerky, but I want you to know that my thoughts and my love are constantly with you.

Lovingly,
Mabel

A Song in the Air— Light in the Darkness

Jim St. Clair

For young David Morrison, living near the spur railway track at Morrison's Siding, Cape Breton, in 1910, the sounds of the various trains were a major part of each day's events. Nearly sightless since his eyes were damaged by a high fever and measles when he was six, now, at age twelve, he delighted in all the sounds around—the far away hopeful promise of the whistle of a train signalling its progress; the clickatey clack of the wheels as the engine and the cars of freight and passenger trains passed rapidly, or the hissing of the brakes as an engineer slowed down to pause on the siding to wait for another train to pass on the single track from Sydney or Point Tupper.

The other sounds of the day pleased him and encouraged him—birds and dogs, his mother singing as she made bread or sorted the mail dropped off from the mail car, his father working in the nearby blacksmith forge, or his three older brothers teasing each other as they came home from school. With only minimal sight David did not attend the nearby one-room school but benefitted from the visits of Mae MacAskill the teacher who came to the Morrison home three times a week.

With a fine singing voice and a strong interest in music, Mae taught David the songs in English and French and Gaelic, both religious and secular. He seemed to be able to see the very notes in his head. David particularly relished the services in the local Presbyterian church, because a wealthy native of Morrison's

Siding, now residing in Boston, had given her former neighbours and relatives a pump organ to accompany the congregational singing of hymns. For David, the slightly reedy sound of the musical instrument was a stimulus which remained with him all week long until the next Sunday. The minister's wife who played the organ encouraged David to run his hands over the keys and try to play notes as she provided the pumping required to push air through the reeds. He wanted to learn more.

As the days of December advanced towards Christmas, David's mother was busy preparing a special Christmas pudding and gingerbread cookies. It was a sad time for her and her family, for only six months earlier word had come from Butte, Montana, that their oldest son and brother Edward had been killed in a mine accident. Only nineteen, he was earning money to help his family at home and to save funds for further education—he wished to train to be a missionary in Africa. He was very close to his youngest brother David whose affliction deeply worried him.

Each time the evening train slowed down as it approached the junction where a hand-operated switch changed the direction of the track so that the train could pause on the siding, Martha Morrison's mind went back to the July evening when not only had the train stopped on the siding, but a large crate containing the casket with the body of Edward was carefully removed from the baggage car by her husband and her brothers. The sound of that evening train still brought her deep anguish.

As darkness settled over the land on this December evening of 1910, the acute ears of David sensed that the train from the Strait of Canso was on its scheduled way along the tracks. A whistle from several miles away and a clanging of the bell signaled that not only would the train go on to the siding but there was freight to be unloaded. The rhythm of the regular beat of the wheels on the tracks set David's feet in motion—his response to sound had always been strong from the time of his infancy but had increased as he learned to inhabit a world which he could see but dimly.

And then, the hiss of the steam escaping from beneath the engine—the wheels squealing on the rails—his father and his brothers and uncles exchanging greetings and jokes with the engineers and conductors. Directions were shouted for unloading the freight—so much to hear and understand. And then nearer and nearer the rumble of the passenger train from Sydney on the main line. Clickety clack—toot of the whistle—clanging of the bell. So much stimulation so much rhythm through his body. David's imagination was already creating a song about trains and journeys to far off places as the Sydney train lumbered past and went off towards the Strait.

And now the starting up of the engine on the siding with its chugs and lugs and creaks and the sound of the switch being turned! Then the exchange of the final words of the folks on the train and those on the platform. At last, the track at Morrison's Siding settled down to the quiet of a December evening.

But with some commotion at the Morrison house. A large wooden box which came on the train was brought into the front hall of the house by David's father and brothers—he could just see the outline—five feet high and six feet long. What could it be? Where did it come from? All were asking questions.

For Martha, the new crate was a poignant reminder of the one which had contained the body of her dear son so recently crushed in a fall of rock. The joyful anticipation of Christmas visitors and a family feast were erased from her mind. Quietly, she wept as her husband and sons opened this unexpected container.

And then. . . . On a dark December evening . . . in a quiet corner of Cape Breton . . . amid a mood of sad remembrance . . . a remarkably ornate parlour organ emerged from the darkness of the packing box—a polished instrument complete with mirror and ivory keys and large golden letters—"Thomas Organ and Piano Company, Woodstock, Ontario."

David's father opened the bill of lading attached to the crate—and read out—"Parlour Organ to be sent in December to David Morrison, Morrison's Siding, Cape Breton, from his brother Edward"—the date ordered?—June 20, 1910, just weeks before Edward's short life came suddenly to an end. His care of his brother and his hope for the lad's future had been much on his heart.

A moment of rebirth . . . of new hope for a nearly blind young man . . . a reminder of the love of a son for his family. . . . Amid the excited comments of his parents and brothers, David went forward and seated himself on the plush-covered organ stool—and began to pump the pedals and tentatively to sound out tunes well cherished in his head—a new experience but one which provided him with a goal in life—to become an accomplished musician, despite his poor sight. And so it is said he did. . . . At Morrison's Siding, darkness turned to light . . . sadness to exhilaration. . . . New hope then and now. . . . As we wish at this season that each of us may hear tunes of old and songs yet to be composed . . . as we strive for new understanding.

Cape Breton Christmas

Stewart Donovan

Brueghel might have seen a reason for
    living in a village like this, with
three small lobster boats buried to the stems;
and only old MacDougall knows
    that the "Ricky and Randy" rots inside
its snow shell.

In the village, wood fires in evening
    light reclaim traditional places

Cape Breton Christmas

smoking slowly in twenty below blue from newly cleaned
chimneys; snow-covered cords of neatly stacked birch and spruce
    steal attention from the hibernating rows
of lobster traps.

On the roofs crows and ravens wait
    for Mary MacDougall's white arm bearing a red bowl
of bread crusts, bacon rinds and dried gingercake
flung far from the steps for crow, raven and gull
    cursed as scavengers. Only the jay
braves the broom to feed on the back porch.

In the Christmas Eve quiet of the vestry
    the newly appointed parish priest
stacks hockey sticks and rolls of tape; Sister
Arsenault smiles at the thought of the eyes of
    the prayer-book receiving boys.

It is now two days since sun and rain flooded
    the forest with silver thaw; no longer naked
the bent birch splits crystal light through
rainbow branches. But Leo Doyle on Christmas call
    knows the reach of silver trees; cracked insulators
and inch-thick ice on the line.

Suppertime brings cold-toed Whitty children home
    to cocoa and brown beans, leaving only
old MacDougall on the ice; he has two dozen now,
smelting since three under his freshly cut fir: one smelt
    every ten minutes entices but his toes too
tell the time.

Five village lamps compete with stars
    as the Doyle children refuse the rides
of their midnight neighbours. Set in snow-covered
spruces the gothic structure echoes with whispers
    at the back where handshakes
jam the doors.

Up front Saint Patrick's statue, returned
    from dust and banishment, glows green
in the Christmas lights of the new-cut crib.
On the granite slopes of Smokey

Leo Doyle unhooks his spurs
As freckled boys shout

"Hockey sticks!" and kitchen lights burn late
    for sleepy mothers with final touches to
turkeys and toys. CBC presents the Queen in
white on channel two (the working one)
    and an unignored storm warning:
at Philip's Nose

the mountain will cut the village off
    (for the night at least) but the storm-stayed
children dream through drifts of forty feet, while
Leo Doyle gets overtime and not so lowly satisfaction
    from the now familiar flash
of the truck's revolving amber light.

Oh, Oh, Oh

Ellison Robertson

I was sixteen at the time of the Santa Claus "scandal." Afterward I didn't have to even pretend anymore to my younger sisters and brother that he existed. Of course I hadn't believed in him since I was five, and when they witnessed the "scandal" they were old enough, my little sister being eight, that they'd already quietly accepted the truth. But afterward there wasn't a kid in town past the age of four or five who didn't give a skeptic's smirk when the jolly old elf was mentioned. It was the parents (well, mothers mainly) and teachers, even in high school, who openly admitted distress at their children's casual loss of faith, at their acceptance of the hollowness of a carefully fostered adult myth.

    I thought it was great, and I was proud that I'd had a small part in the whole thing, my father having volunteered me as a sort of Santa's helper. Not that I hadn't tried to get out of it. I mean, I'd already gotten my hands on the *Freewheelin' Bob Dylan* and the first Mothers of Invention albums. Revolution was in the air, sort of, even in a Cape Breton mining town, and if we were going to tear down the past, Santa Claus was as good a place as any to begin. Politics could come later.

There were special parent-teacher meetings called, and sermons in most of the churches, but the harm, as they saw it, had already been done. Kids my age learned to keep our comments and even our laughter to ourselves, or expect a rambling lecture about joy and faith and innocence and the pain of growing up too soon that could leave us with the guilty sense of being accomplices in some heinous crime against humanity. The little kids were treated that Christmas as if they'd contracted some horrible terminal illness, as if they'd never see another December 25th in this world.

But then none of this is going to make any sense unless I tell you what happened and give you a little bit of the background.

Each year since the late Forties, about a week before Christmas, the local Legion had sponsored a visit from Santa Claus. I've been told that the first few years he'd arrive by sleigh (a big black one which older kids said looked suspiciously like one that the priest kept in the barn behind the glebe), though it was pulled by a single horse—with deer antlers strapped to its head—rather than by eight reindeer. This practice was abandoned because one year, after being startled by the excited rush of youngsters, the horse bolted and ran like hell for the dairy stables. A few small kids were trampled by older ones in the panic. Luckily no one was run down by the horse itself, though Santa was thrown from the sleigh and, with blood streaming from a broken nose, fired off an amazing catalogue of curses. Then for a few years, until it lost a runner and had to be carted in the bed of the truck, the sleigh was pulled into the schoolyard by the pickup. There's a photograph of me, at the age of three, sitting on my father's shoulder and watching Santa arrive in this fashion. My father's face bears a wide-eyed, rum-inspired look of excitement, while mine is averted in terror.

At four, I waded in with the rest, desperate for my share of the candy and the small toys it was rumoured were handed out on a first-come basis. I managed, through the generous assistance of a bigger boy, to get my hands on a small wooden boat, its soot-streaked sails suggesting that Santa had rescued it from the temporary discount toy store that had recently burned down in North Sydney. At five, I was bold enough to climb into the sleigh to sit on Santa's lap and tell him what I hoped against hope to receive on Christmas morning.

This is one of my most vivid early memories, and yet it isn't all that clear, if you know what I mean, being tainted over the years by retelling, first by my parents and eventually by me. I don't remember what I thought or how I worked it out, for instance, but I know that I realized in an instant that this wasn't Santa Claus. I was secure upon his broad knee, wrapped in the heavy comfort of his red-velveted arms, when I was suddenly aware of a funky odour of stale smoke, an unwashed body and sour, alcohol-tainted breath. I peered up into Santa's eyes and saw that they weren't crinkled and twinkling but rather bloodshot and baggy. I pressed my mittened palms against his bulging belly and felt the padding, as saggy and misplaced as the stuffing of our old sofa at home. I started to cry, squirmed out of his grasp, heard the appalling rasp of his laughter behind me as I jumped from the sleigh.

It wasn't Santa Claus. It was Cecil Morrison, a sad, crumpled man my father sometimes talked to, giving him whatever change he had in his pockets, as we strolled on the main street, a man who had been in our house a few times, who'd sat drinking rum in the kitchen, railing on about things I didn't understand until late at night when I'd heard the clatter of him stumbling out into the darkness.

I don't recall how I worked it out, but by the following year I knew there wasn't a Santa, that "poor Cecil," as my mother called him when I ventured to share the revelation of our Santa's identity, was as close to real as this curious fantasy ever came. I suppose I deduced this because I'd taken the first step on the Jesuits' slippery slope away from faith (assuming it applies to matters not quite religious), because, as they asserted, the entirety of even the greatest Mystery could be unravelled from the doubter's gentlest tug upon a single thread of the whole cloth of belief.

At first I was sorry to know the truth, though in succeeding years it didn't seem to matter. I still looked forward to the event, joined my friends' excited rush to surround the pickup truck—I think the sleigh was dispensed with altogether by 1955—and happily received my share of sweets.

When I speak of our excitement, I'm not simply indulging in nostalgic memory of the youthful intensity of feeling any one of you might attribute to your childhood. For those growing up in more recent decades, or even for those of my age and older who were raised in different circumstances, the importance of this modest annual event might be difficult to grasp. We generally had so little. Not that we were always unhappily conscious of this; we simply clung to the preciousness of whatever we received and modestly hoped for more. I'm not sure how one completely measures such things, but I'm certain, as I look about me thirty years later, that in many important ways things in this town are decidedly worse than they were. There's little work, and so hope is even more scarce.

However, just as it is everywhere these days, there is an over-abundance of desire. Kids have cable TV and video games and computers and—well, you know the line—but even the youngest now may see Santa Claus as no more than one more huckster feeding their insecurity about the things they can't have. What I'm trying to say is that only now does it occur to me how much my teenage skepticism made me their forebear. In contrast, my parents' cultivated innocence wasn't so much naive as it was, perhaps, a necessary bulwark against their own harsh upbringing during years of depression and war.

The men who belonged to the Legion, like my father, had almost all been in combat during one of the World Wars, and they'd come home to work in the pit or at other equally tough labour. If they didn't prosper, they nonetheless embraced the promise of simply living, working and producing families. The Legion was a social club, usually a place to drink without the censuring gaze of the women, but it had to serve higher purposes too. It sponsored baseball and hockey teams, raised money for the needy, set up scholarships, and so on and so on. And it arranged for the visit of Santa Claus each December.

These were the men whose example taught me to see in certain forms of toughness a special susceptibility to sentimentality. Each year they employed Cecil in the role, one of the few paying jobs he was offered, as an honourable form of charity to make sure his own family had a little money for the holidays. Cecil was a veteran; enough said. But he was also a drunk, a man nearly destroyed by the burden of what we think of as ordinary life.

I don't know how Cecil came to be Santa Claus. His wife made the costume for him and perhaps that was all it took. He was only in his late twenties when he began, still vigorous and enthusiastic and with enough sense to put off drinking until after the candy was handed out. Even by the late Fifties, though, he was pretty far gone. The other men knew they had to keep an eye on him for a few days prior to the event; they'd stop buying him booze, and they never, never paid him until the children were dispersed and everyone had adjourned to the Legion bar. Oh, and they held back most of the money to give to his wife a couple of days before Christmas so he wouldn't spend it all in one go.

What tipped the balance finally and precipitated the "scandal" was the election of a newcomer to the job of treasurer; that and the fact that no one thought to explain about Cecil and the money. As I'd learned from listening to my father talking to my mother over the years, it was their practice each year to insist that Cecil show up at the Legion by nine on the appointed Saturday morning. That way they could assess his condition, feed him a couple of curative beers if need be, and then pour coffee into him until noon, when he was scheduled to make his entrance on the school grounds.

That fateful December morning, when Cecil hadn't shown up by ten, my father began phoning people to try and track down the errant Santa. He quickly learned about the money. I happened to be at the Legion delivering a box of bagged candy that my mother had put together, preparing it late at night so my younger siblings wouldn't know. I'd tried to tell her they already knew the truth, but she'd given me one of her disappointed looks and I'd shut up. It was when my father managed to reach a neighbour of Cecil's, who ran next door to fetch Cecil's wife, Rhodena, that the men were pushed to the brink of panic. She said Cecil hadn't come home at all the night before.

"Can't someone else dress up as Santa Claus?" I asked, adding with my best sixteen-year-old sarcasm, "I mean, it isn't exactly Shakespeare."

The six or seven men, my father included, turned upon me as one with looks that might have threatened physical mayhem. But then my father said quietly, and I like to think proudly, "He's right." I came that close to being the hero of the day. There was a brief discussion as to who would make a suitable Santa, each of them doing his best to nominate someone else, before my father suddenly remembered Cecil's wife was still on the line. "Rhodena," he said, "you still there? Listen, we'll have a look for Cecil but if we can't find him or if he's . . . well, we'll just come and get the Santa Claus suit." He listened then for a moment, his frown deepening, then nearly shouted, "*What!* Damn. Okay, we'll find him." He dropped the receiver onto its cradle with distaste, then turned the same dour grimace on me, as if I was somehow to blame.

The long and the short of it was that Cecil not only had been paid the day before but had been given the keys to the already decorated pickup. And he'd left home after supper with the money, truck and Santa's outfit. Once these facts were absorbed and the inevitable product of the equation silently acknowledged, the men swung into action with admirable military precision.

They called every member of the Legion, every tavern, club and bootlegger. They sent out scouting parties, including a group of teens they insisted I organize. I grew steadily more excited, feeling as close as I'd yet been to the status of an adult, though each time I checked in my father and his friends seemed to be struggling less successfully against the gloomy admission of the fruitlessness of the search. Even the town police and the nearby Mountie detachment were alerted to widen the manhunt. All to no avail. Santa's visit would have to be postponed.

A few men began to mutter imprecations against Cecil, as if he alone were responsible. By eleven-thirty they'd despaired of finding him and begun looking daggers at the treasurer, who felt he had to show up but had wisely kept to himself in a corner of the bar. No doubt under the goad of their seething resentment, he suddenly had an inspiration. "The Rotary Club," he burst out in a hoarse, emotional cry, and was looked at sullenly by the crowd, which numbered a couple of dozen by then, more than enough for a lynching. Composing himself, he explained that the Rotary Club in North Sydney put on a Christmas party every year. They'd held it the week before and one of the members had played Santa Claus. Within fifteen minutes he'd located the man by phone and arranged for him to get right over to our town, a drive of maybe twenty minutes. Of course, he had to get into his costume, which would take maybe twenty or twenty-five minutes more because it was at the club. The treasurer was suddenly elevated to the role of hero. The mood of the room swung dramatically upward. This called for a celebration, so beers were handed round and hoisted with cheers.

Not one to be easily distracted from the practical, my father thoughtfully sipped at his beer, his eyebrows dipping in calculation, and announced that the best they could hope for was that Santa Claus would reach the school by quarter to one. This was when he volunteered my services. I'd bought a guitar the year before and had recently formed a folk group. We wanted to be a rock group but hadn't found a drummer. Since all four of us were present, he suggested we be dispatched to the school to announce Santa's delay and play Christmas carols until he showed.

"We don't know any Christmas carols," I whined, turning my back on any pretension to being an adult, but he waved this objection aside. "Everyone knows some carols, and you can sing that other stuff you're always practicing, 'Row your boat in the wind, Michael' or whatever."

Though I opened my mouth again to protest, I didn't get a word out before he said firmly, "No buts!" He did slip each of us five dollars as we sulkily headed out the door.

Once outside, I feared the other guys might just take off. Instead Melvin, the other guitar player, kissed his five and said, "Our first paid gig, boys. Fame and fortune, here we come."

We ran to get the guitars and met back at the school only a few minutes after twelve. We pushed our way through the crowd of about a hundred, kids of all ages and a scattering of adults who'd brought little kids. The sight of us on the school steps with our guitars was enough to get their attention, though most of them eyed us with sour suspicion. I'd been elected to make the announcements, and I did so in a high wavering pitch of nervousness. I don't think most of them heard me, but the news rippled back through the crowd and everyone pressed closer. We ran through "Jingle Bells" and a bit of "Good King Wenceslas" before we had to fall back on the Kingston Trio and Bob Dylan tunes we'd been learning. We were forced soon to begin repeating the songs and saw quickly the stirring of rebellion on the young faces below us. Then Mr. Larsen, the music teacher from our high school, stepped forward, climbed the steps to stand beside us, and sang just about every carol known to man, while we pretended to accompany him with the three or four chords we knew. Finally, even his presence wasn't enough, and I saw that some of the older boys at the fringe of the gathering were beginning to make snowballs.

Custer wouldn't have welcomed reinforcements any more than we did the sudden gleeful cry of a little girl at the back of the crowd, "Santa's comin', Santa's comin'." The pickup rolled to a stop and was surrounded. The North Sydney Santa waved and a cheer went up. Everyone was beaming, but I thought with an odd sense of resentment of how he was showing up our Santa. Even in memory I knew Cecil's suit was pretty seedy now in comparison, the errant padding barely filling out his scrawny frame. This guy was actually fat, and his beard looked almost real.

He ho, ho, ho-ed a lot and sat on the tailgate to receive the lists of the smaller children, and he was just getting down to the serious attraction of the day, passing out candy, games and small toys, when a second truck squealed up the drive, adorned with ribbons, bows, and bedraggled Kleenex flowers. Everyone scattered and the pickup halted just short of a collision with the North Sydney Santa's vehicle. A second Santa, minus hat, stringy beard askew, rolled from the driver's seat and staggered sideways before he regained a semblance of balance and advanced unsteadily toward the new Santa. "My friggin' job, b'y," he howled and raised his fists to the sky. "Y . . . y . . . yyyou *impostor*!" Somebody shouted, "You tell 'im Cecil," and a slow ragged chant began, gaining force until even the smallest were crying out, "Go Cecil, go Cecil, go Cecil. . . ."

And Cecil went. With astounding agility considering his condition, he leapt onto the pickup and grabbed the other Santa by the throat. Kids were hollering, "Get him," "Nail him," "Pound him, Cecil," and the few adults, mostly men, torn between amusement and embarrassment, seemed to be edging away. Then, as the two Santas stomped about, looking more like dancers than two men fighting, the bags of candy, games and toys were kicked over and spilled onto the snow-crusted pavement. All hell broke loose, as they say, as the kids surged forward, squirming, shoving and diving to grab up the spoils of this minor battle.

By then word had somehow spread and the men from the Legion arrived, many of them having added five or six beers to the glow they liked to maintain through the several weeks up to and including the holiday season. They waded in, though it looked more like they were siding with one or the other of the Santas rather than trying to subdue them. Soon enough, though, they were worn out, standing about red-faced with exhaustion and shame, while both of the Santas lay gasping in the truck like a couple of beached whales.

In the midst of the melee, the police chief had arrived, simply putting in his usual formal appearance but suddenly called on to restore law and order. Barely suppressing his laughter, he wrestled the red-suited antagonists from the truck and pushed them into the back of the cruiser, where they continued limply swatting at each other. The chief looked about at the astonished collection of moon-faced youngsters who stood round the car, clutching handfuls of goodies. He laughed finally and said, "Don't worry, kids, I'll find out which one of these guys is the real Santa and let him go before Christmas Eve."

The departure of the black-and-white police car signalled the end of the spectacle. The adults had all slunk off, most of them back to the Legion, and those my age were already retelling the story to each other, over and over. Once we'd exhausted the variations that were possible from our differing points of view, we hurried off to find any of our acquaintances unlucky enough to have missed it. All that remained to complete the legend was for the mothers to hear the tale and title it "The Scandal in the Schoolyard," and the aftermath of that I've already described.

Now I'm older than my father was that Christmas. I'm an adult, for better or worse, with grown children of my own. Over the years I've told this story countless times, though always as a joke and always mindful of the laughter I'd incite. Writing it down, I find it necessary to admit the element of tragedy which lies closer to the comic than we often care to recognize.

The Legion never sponsored the event again. Cecil never played Santa again, though his Legion buddies found other small ways to employ him in their good works. The year following the "scandal," the manager of the five-and-dime store hired someone else to play Santa. Of course I wouldn't be caught dead going in to check him out, though I heard he just took the kids' wish lists and pointed out to the parents anything on them that was for sale in the store; there was no more candy given away.

I suppose I've grown old enough to turn sentimental in my own way as the world rolls on, and now when I recall that long-ago Christmas, I inevitably think of another. When my daughter was six, I was in my mid-thirties. It was less than a week before Christmas. I sat with a group of friends, drinking and trying to one-up each other with memories of our families' Christmas peculiarities—the subject itself a sort of compendium of "Christmases from hell," and each narrator a self-styled curmudgeon, the Christmas wounded, bravely if cynically trying to survive another one. I told a few stories, all the while carefully building up to the tale of the battling Santas.

Careless of my daughter's presence, I offered it to the expected gleeful laughter. With the sureness of a middle-aged iconoclast, I even smiled at her thoughtful, troubled gaze. Several days later, as I beamed happily down upon her as she ripped open a present on which the card read, "Love from Santa," she paused to look back at me with her deep, far-seeing blue eyes and announced, "Daddy, I don't believe anymore in Santa Claus, the Easter Bunny, or God."

Cape Breton Homes Go All Out With Christmas Decorations

Greg MacNeil

Memories of Christmas past are the inspiration for some of the larger Christmas decorating displays around Cape Breton this year, and their creators are hoping their extensive holiday handiwork will create more memories for the people who stop to enjoy them.

"I attribute all of this to my own mother and father. When we were kids they used to take us around to places," said Blair Melanson, whose Cottage Road setup includes music streamed to your car radio, a hologram of Santa Claus and a nativity scene, among many other things.

"There was a gentleman on Hardwood Hill who had a big display and he gave it to the park when he died. We used to go there every year when we were kids."

Melanson started his own display twenty-nine years ago and has been adding to it each year to make it more enjoyable for his family and the many other families who stop by to view it.

"A little fellow was here, two years old, looking at Santa in the window. He couldn't take his eyes off of him. They come and a lot of them take pictures up front with Minnie Mouse and Goofy."

The thousands of lights that make up his display include 7,000 alone on a big tree in his front yard and another 4,000 on several arches.

"The first stuff I ever bought was at Newman's Hardware in the Pier and then I just continued on from there. Seven years ago I started doing Light-o-Rama—the blinking lights and computerized controls."

On George Street, Kim Cooke and her husband Dan Webb are well known for their extensive Halloween decorations and have recently added Christmas to the fun.

As a result, the glow of the lights wrapped around trees, fences and Hello Kitty and Peanuts decorations can be seen from afar.

"We've been building it just like Halloween and adding a bit every year," said Cooke. "Next year we are going to be building a gingerbread house in the summertime."

She said their five children enjoy the growing holiday decorating tradition, as do the many people who drive to their front yard to see it each night.

Many people have been making the drive to Port Morien this year, as well, to check out the second-year efforts of Loren Pemberton, whose 9,000-light display is synched to music through an elaborate computer program.

"The programming for the sequences involves taking a song and trying to get the highlights of the song to mesh with the beats or the melody of the song," said Pemberton. "It can take a long time. A three-minute song can take upwards of twenty or thirty hours work."

When that music is broadcast to visitors through a small FM transmitter with a range of a few hundred feet, completely in sync with his light display, "It's a riot."

Pemberton said, "Sometimes if I add a new song or change something, I've overheard some great conversations. It's pretty funny. The other night I had a couple of young kids dancing at the end of the driveway."

Like other large displays, Pemberton said his is a year-round effort. Despite the work, he does it for the obvious joy it gives others and to honour childhood memories of visiting large displays in Glace Bay.

"Seeing Christmas through the eyes of kids has been a wonderful re-invention of Christmas for me. It's pretty nice and gives me and the kids a lot of fun."

A can of popcorn and a thank-you card from a teen, and a nice note dropped in his mailbox, are some of the reasons why Jim Deleski continues to brighten the yard of his Elmbank Avenue home in Sydney year after year.

"That's the part that makes it all worthwhile," Deleski said. "The feedback we've gotten from all our neighbours is that they love it. I'm glad people enjoy it. That's really what it is all about."

Christmas in Wentworth Park is among his favourite childhood memories, and it continues to inspire a display that has grown from a 16-channel controller and 5,000 lights to over 30,000 lights and many new types of technology.

"One controller is on the big tree in the middle of my yard where I can control each individual lightbulb. I can now control the colour of each light."

An FM radio broadcast is part of his display, too.

Despite the expense and hard work, Deleskie, Melanson, Cooke and Pemberton plan to continue sharing their displays during the Christmas season as they make memories for their countless nightly visitors.

"It's nice that people comment on how much they like it," said Melanson. "People come back with their own kids now. There was one here not long ago who said she remembered coming here as a kid. Now she's coming back with her own son. It's nice to hear that."

Acknowledgements
continued from page iv:

"Better Not Pout" is published with the permission of the author Jordan MacVay. "Our First Christmas" is taken from *The Woman from Away* by Tessie Gillis (Breton Books). "The chaos, the cussing . . . it must be Christmas" by Ann Dempsey is reprinted with permission of Torstar Syndication Services. "Old Santa Claus, 1918" is from *Days That I Remember* by Francis MacGregor (Lancelot Press). "A Christmas Story" is reprinted with permission from the *Velo Cape Breton Newsletter*. "Cape Breton Homes Go All Out With Christmas Decorations" by staff writer Greg MacNeil; "I am finally getting the Christmas spirit" by columnist Verna Murphy; and "Christmas Island Christmas," by travel writer Andrea Sachs—originally published as "Have Yourself a Nova Scotia Christmas"—were all published in the *Cape Breton Post*.

"The Christmas of 1953" is published with permission of Marie Battiste. Jack O'Donnell of The Men of the Deeps first brought us the story of "Christmas in the Coal Mine—An Initiation," a performance of which can be seen at https://www.youtube.com/watch?v=yDZLT-bQqMY. Our thanks to Joanne Watts and the Chestico Museum, Port Hood, for "Coming Home for Christmas—1943." Dan Doucet brought us Elsie Aucoin Frontain's "The Christmas Concert." The Mabel Bell letters are courtesy the Alexander Graham Bell National Historic Site; our thanks to Valerie Mason and Rosalynd Ingraham. "Sandy's Cape Breton Pork Pies" was found on the web at http://www.piepalace.ca/blog/2007/12/sandys-cape-breton-pork-pies.html. Rosie Aucoin Grace's story of "The $25,000 Acadian Meat Pie and *Le Réveillon*" appeared in *The Inverness Oran*. "The Christmas Dorothy Died" is from Wanda Robson's book *Sister to Courage* (Breton Books).

"A Curtis Family Memory," "Christmas in the First World War," "Christmas on Long Island," "Remembering D.W. MacLeod," "Oidhche Na Calluinn," "Hong Kong Fell on Christmas Day, 1941," "Christmas on Scatarie Island," "Mi'kmaq Memories," "Fighting for the Light," "When They Arrested Santa Claus," "A Christmastime Walk" and "A Memory of Ironville" are from *Cape Breton's Magazine*.

"Christmas Without Dickens" is from Hugh MacLennan's *Thirty & Three*, with permission The Estate of Hugh MacLennan and McGill Queen's University Press. "Beannachdan na Nollaig Oirbh!" was collected and translated by Seamus Watson and first published in *Am Braighe*; it is available at the Highland Village Museum website, https://highlandvillage.novascotia.ca/gaelic-nova-scotia/our-stories.

"A Child's Christmas Day Diary, 1914" is from Ella Liscombe's diary, MG 12/59 Beaton Institute, Cape Breton University. David Frank supplied "Nova Scotia's $1.38-a-Day Laborer and His Family"; it was published in 1906 in *The Halifax Herald* and *The Labor Herald*. "Merry Christmas to You, Jim" appears in *Echoes from Labor's Wars* by Dawn Fraser (Breton Books). "Archie Neil Chisholm's Christmas Present" is from *Archie Neil: From the Life and Stories of Archie Neil Chisholm of Margaree Forks* by Mary Anne Ducharme (Breton Books). "A Latvian Immigrant's Note of Thanks" was found on the Canadian Museum of Immigration Pier 21 website: http://www.pier21.ca/stories/latvian-immigrant-andris-kundzins.

Cape Breton's Christmas

"A Jewish Child's Christmas in Cape Breton" is published with permission of the Estate of Joseph Sherman and Ann Sherman; "I remember Lon and footsteps in the snow" with permission of Kenneth Bagnell; and "Christmas Tails" with permission of Maureen MacIntosh. Jim St. Clair provided the text for his "A Song in the Air—Light in the Darkness." "One Christmas Eve in the Korean War" by Roly Soper is from *The Korean Newsletter War Veteran Internet Journal*, at http://www.kvacanada.com/newsletterpdf/Dec242011newsletter.pdf. The poem "Cape Breton Christmas" is from Stewart Donovan's *Cape Breton Quarry* (Breton Books). Ellison Robertson's "Oh, oh, oh" is from his book of short stories called *The Last Gael* (Breton Books). Our thanks, as well, to Fr. Roman Dusanowskyj and Paul MacDougall for their contributions to *Cape Breton's Christmas*.